Community-Led Regeneration

Community-Led Regeneration

A Toolkit for Residents and Planners

Pablo Sendra and Daniel Fitzpatrick

First published in 2020 by
UCL Press
University College London
Gower Street
London WC1E 6BT

Available to download free: www.uclpress.co.uk

A CIP catalogue record for this book is available from The British Library.

ISBN: 978-1-78735-608-5 (Hbk.)
ISBN: 978-1-78735-607-8 (Pbk.)
ISBN: 978-1-78735-606-1 (PDF)
ISBN: 978-1-78735-609-2 (epub)
ISBN: 978-1-78735-610-8 (mobi)
DOI: https://doi.org/10.14324/111.9781787356061

Contents

List of figures

List of abbreviations

CARP	Carpenters Against Regeneration Plans
CGC	Cressingham Gardens Community
CLSA	Conditional Land Sale Agreement
CLT	Community Land Trust
EU	European Union
FOI	Freedom of Information
GCNF	Greater Carpenters Neighbourhood Forum
GLA	Greater London Authority
HRA	Housing Revenue Account
JR	Judicial Review
LA 2011	Localism Act 2011
LBN	London Borough of Newham
LLDC	London Legacy Development Corporation
LTF	London Tenants Federation
NDC	New Deal for Communities
NFTMO	National Federation of Tenant Management Organisations
NP	Neighbourhood Plan
PEACH	People's Empowerment Alliance for Custom House
RSL	Registered Social Landlord
RtM	Right to Manage
RtT	Right to Transfer
SPD	Supplementary Planning Document
SRB	Single Regeneration Budget
TMO	Tenant Management Organisation
UCL	University College London
WEAG	Walterton and Elgin Action Group
WECH	Walterton and Elgin Community Homes
WKGG	West Kensington and Gibbs Green
WKGGCH	West Ken Gibbs Green Community Homes

List of contributors

Authors

Daniel Fitzpatrick is Teaching Fellow and researcher at The Bartlett School of Planning, UCL. His doctoral research was on mutual housing models in London and their governance. He has been researching the relationship between community groups and universities in planning, and looking at formal and informal practices of estate regeneration and collective housing. He has worked in India, Italy, Cuba, Chile, Nepal and London, working on projects at different scales – from international development and within local government. He was a founding partner of the planning and architecture practice Variant Office between 2014 and 2018.

Dr Pablo Sendra is Lecturer in Planning and Urban Design at The Bartlett School of Planning, UCL. He combines his academic career with professional practice in urban design. He is co-founder of the urban design practice Lugadero, which has recently facilitated a co-design process for two public spaces in Wimbledon, London. He is also co-founder of CivicWise, a network promoting civic engagement and collaborative urbanism. He develops action research projects and radical teaching in collaboration with community groups and activists in London. At UCL, Sendra is the Director of the MSc in Urban Design and City Planning programme, the coordinator of the Civic Design CPD course and the Deputy Leader of the Urban Design Research Group. He is co-author (with Richard Sennett) of *Designing Disorder* (forthcoming) and co-editor (with Maria J. Pita and CivicWise) of *Civic Practices* (2017). He is part of the City Collective for the journal *City*.

Other contributors

Michael Edwards studied economics, then planning, at UCL 1964–6. He worked in Nathaniel Lichfield's practice, doing economic inputs to the Plan for Milton Keynes. He has enjoyed lecturing at The Bartlett School, UCL since 1969 and been involved in all the Examinations in Public (EiPs) on London Plans since 2000, working with the network of community groups Just Space (justspace.org.uk). His publications are at michaeledwards.org.uk and he tweets as @michaellondonsf. His 2015 paper on housing, rent and land over the next 45 years, commissioned by the Government Office for Science Foresight project on the future of UK cities, is at http://bit.ly/1NvjmV7. He is semi-retired.

Richard Lee is the coordinator of Just Space, a London-wide network of community and voluntary groups operating at the local and city-wide level. It came together in 2007 to influence the strategic (spatial) plan for London – the London Plan. The Just Space network has brought together and nurtured a huge amount of experience and knowledge from London's diverse community organisations. This has been channelled into making policy proposals for a fair and sustainable London. Universities have played an important role in supporting the work of Just Space, meeting the needs of community groups through research, teaching, student volunteering and the free use of university space. Just Space publications include *Towards a Community-Led Plan for London* (2016) and *Social Impact Assessment in London Planning* (2018).

Sarah Sackman is a practising public interest barrister specialising in public and planning law. She is a housing and community campaigner and has acted for tenants and residents groups fighting for fairer regeneration, and for public bodies and the housing charity Shelter to deliver more social housing. Sarah holds degrees from Cambridge and Harvard universities and teaches human rights and planning law as a Visiting Lecturer at the London School of Economics (and UCL).

Preface

Richard Lee and Michael Edwards, Just Space

In cities around the world the pressure of 'investment' in search of rents and profits is displacing low-income citizens and local economic activities, disrupting lives and livelihoods and often demolishing existing homes in the process. London is distinctive in two main ways: it is a huge, unequal and expensive city to live in and it has a strong heritage of council housing. As the largest city in Europe, the capital of one of Europe's most unequal nations, London has a housing market with very high rents and prices compared with incomes. It is often referred to simultaneously as a wealth machine and a poverty machine.

Thanks to campaigns for better housing during the nineteenth and twentieth centuries, the UK developed a system of council housing. Municipalities (including the London County Council and its successor, the Greater London Council) were allowed to build and manage housing for their residents. The more progressive councils did so, and the proportion of households living in so-called 'social housing' (council plus housing association housing) rose to one-third of the population in England and Wales in 1981; the proportion in London was slightly higher. Since then the social sector has shrunk through the Right to Buy initiative and other losses, while councils have been forbidden from building and constrained even in doing maintenance.

Council housing offered secure tenancies to diverse populations of London workers, with strong concentrations in central and inner London where Labour councils had been the most active builders. With the intensification of speculative developer pressure since the 1990s, pressure has mounted on councils to demolish and replace council estates with flats for the open market – and, to some extent, replacements for existing tenants. The social violence of these estate demolitions has made them the quintessential planning issue of twenty-first century London.

Just Space is a London-wide network of community groups which came into existence to foster mutual support on the London-wide planning of the new Greater London Authority (GLA). We see planning in a very broad sense and we cover many issues, but the issue that has gained most attention from us over the years is so-called 'estate regeneration'. Or, put another way, the protection of council estates, which have been under threat of demolition for a long time now. We are very clear that we stand with working-class communities whose rights to the city have been strongly challenged. Five years ago, in 2014, Just Space, working with London Tenants Federation and others, produced two guides. Together with Loretta Lees, we wrote *Staying Put: An Anti-Gentrification Handbook* for council estates in London. This includes the stories of the Carpenters Community Plan and Walterton and Elgin Community Homes, among others.

We also worked with Sarah Bell and the Engineering Exchange at UCL on *Demolition or Refurbishment of Social Housing? A Review of the Evidence*. Alongside this were three fact sheets – on embodied carbon, lifespan of a building, health and wellbeing – and a community toolkit. Both of these can be found on the Just Space website, http://www.justspace.org.uk, along with other publications about our work.

What about now? Has there been any change? The Mayor of London's *Guidance on Estate Regeneration* is a welcome shift in the direction of tenants' and leaseholders' rights but is let down by exemptions and limitations, which Just Space and others have opposed. We argue that councils should be obliged always to ballot their tenants and residents on any demolition plan. We disagree that it should only apply where the development has funding from the Mayor. On the contrary: it has to be a planning policy matter. Nor can this apply only to larger schemes.

Just Space and its member organisations are not just defensive: we constantly emphasise the deep, rich knowledge of estates and localities among residents and the great contribution which residents – organised and resourced – can make to the care and (genuine) regeneration of their areas. Proposals for this kind of community-led regeneration were central in our 2016 work, *Towards a Community-Led Plan for London*. Well before the Grenfell Tower outrage occurred, this document placed the maintenance and upgrading of existing housing as top priority.

In March 2019, as part of the Examination in Public (EiP) of the London Plan, there was a session on estate regeneration which heard evidence from London Tenants Federation, London Forum, Footwork Architects (ft'work), Just Space and others. The draft London Plan still implies a default position of demolition, and estate regeneration still seems to mean knocking down rather than doing up. We made clear statements to protect council estates against demolition and displacement, urging for far higher levels of community engagement from the earliest stage. Some small gains seem to have been extracted from the GLA, but we await the Inspector's Report to see what impact our arguments carry. It is a long and continuing struggle.

This book is important because it documents some of the struggles in which London tenants and residents have defended their homes and communities, and demonstrates how good the outcomes can – or could – be. Each threat to a London locality generates solidarity and support from across the city; this book is a valuable part of sharing and building our collective knowledge.

Acknowledgements

This book is an output of the research project 'Community-led social housing regeneration: between the formal and the informal', funded by a British Academy/Leverhulme Small Research Grant. We would like to thank the funders of this research for their support. We would also like to thank our institution University College London, The Bartlett School of Planning, and the professional services staff for their support in managing this funding. We would like to thank UCL Press, in particular commissioning editor Chris Penfold, our copy-editor Catherine Bradley and the anonymous reviewers of the book proposal and manuscript for their support, and for providing us the opportunity of publishing this book in Open Access.

The project has been developed in collaboration with the London-wide network of community organisations Just Space. We would like to thank Just Space for their input on the research. In particular, we would like to thank Richard Lee and Michael Edwards, authors of the Preface of the book, for their contribution to the project. We would also like to thank the barrister Sarah Sackman for agreeing to write chapter 11 on 'Using the law and challenging redevelopment through the courts'.

The project has also had an invaluable contribution from residents, volunteers and professionals supporting community organisations from the seven case studies discussed in this book. In addition to agreeing to be interviewed for the project, they have also agreed to participate in our workshops and to review the texts of the chapters for their case studies; their further suggestions have been really helpful. We would like to thank Jonathan Rosenberg (community organiser of WKGGCH and Chair of WECH) and Harold Greatwood (resident of West Kensington and Gibbs Green and director of WKGGCH), as well as the two housing organisers of WKGGCH who also participated in conversations related to this project (Zoe Savory and Andrew Ward), Ella Bradbury (volunteer at Focus E15), Saskia O'Hara (campaigner at Focus E15), two residents from Cressingham Gardens, Ashvin de Vos (Variant Office), Geraldine

Dening (Architects for Social Housing), Dan Barron (community organiser of PEACH), one of the founder members of PEACH, Elena Besussi and Elizabeth Knowles (residents of Alexandra and Ainsworth Estates), Julian Cheyne (supporter of GCNF) and the resident of Carpenters Estate who spoke in our final event for their input into our research. While finishing this book, we were shocked by the news that Focus E15 volunteer Ella Bradbury had died on 6 September 2019 at the age of 29 in Mexico City. We send our condolences to her family and friends.

We would like too to thank Tom Chance, Victor Adegbuyi and Stephen Hill for their suggestions on some of the parts of this book and Emanuele Belotti and Mara Ferreri for their important reflections on what is happening in other cities in Europe. We are also grateful to Stefano Portelli, a scholar-activist working on similar issues at an international level, who provided useful contextual comments and references in the final stages of drafting the book. We would also like to thank Iqbal Hamiduddin for his valuable comments on the book.

The contribution made by those who participated in our workshops co-organised with Just Space has been also very important. In November 2017 we co-organised a workshop with Just Space around the consultation on the Mayor of London's Draft Housing Strategy. Within that workshop we organised a specific workshop on 'Community-Led Estate Regeneration'. Around 25 people came to this event and contributed to the discussion, which included questions that helped shape the content of this book. In June 2019 we co-organised with Just Space the final workshop for this research project in Gibbs Green Community Hall, in which around 80 people participated. In the workshop, we gave a report of the research project to participants, inviting residents, people supporting residents, and scholars to present the initial findings. We then organised four discussion groups around four topics, the results of which are reflected in Part III of this book. We would like to thank Richard Lee, Becky Turner, Elena Besussi, Frances Brill and Jonathan Rosenberg for helping us in the planning and facilitating of these four discussion topics during the workshops, as well as Cecilia Colombo for helping us by taking notes in one of the workshops. We are also grateful to Andrew Ward for helping with the final event. We would in addition like to thank Loretta Lees, Adam Elliot-Cooper, Joe Penny, Elizabeth Knowles, who spoke about Alexandra Road Park Heritage Lottery Fund restoration, and the residents and community organisers who contributed to the sessions, including those from WKGG, PEACH, Cressingham Gardens, Greater Carpenters Neighbourhood Forum, Alexandra and Ainsworth Estates, and WECH for their participation on the panel sessions. We would like to thank Just Space for co-organising the workshop with us, WKGGCH for hosting us in the community hall and all participants for their contribution to the discussion and the workshops. In addition to this, we would like to thank our students from a range of courses at The Bartlett School of Planning which were taught in collaboration with community organisations; that learning experience has also been important for this piece of research.

Personal acknowledgements from Pablo Sendra: I would like to thank my partner Diana Salazar, my son Índigo, my parents Juanjo and Concha, my sisters Estrella and Carmen and my brother Luis. Their personal support is always essential for completing my research.

Personal acknowledgements from Daniel Fitzpatrick: I would like to thank my parents Ana and Michael, my brother Ian, and Sarah my partner. All have been patient, encouraging and supportive in their unique ways, especially during the editing process.

Introduction

Engaging communities in regeneration processes is vital both for avoiding a displacement of residents and for giving communities the opportunity to take the lead on their neighbourhood's future. Over the last few years different approaches to planning, types of frameworks, regulations and policies have been put in place with the aim of providing communities with formal planning tools for engaging in future developments of their neighbourhood. At the same time, community organisations are using diverse approaches – including direct actions or campaigning, as well as engagement with these formal planning tools – to fight against the demolition of social housing, instead proposing alternative plans that respond more directly to the local community's needs and demands. Despite the availability of such planning tools, some communities encounter many barriers when attempting to influence meaningfully the future of their neighbourhoods, with local authorities often disregarding residents' proposals.

The research that has led to this book has followed campaigns in London and all cases explored in Part I are from this city. In terms of its planning system, London has had in recent years a certain level of autonomy, which currently differs from any other city in England. However, we show that the cases and tools also have a relevance to other city-regions in England and the UK – and indeed are relevant at a global level too. This applies not just to the planning tools, but also to the actual stories and experiences of communities who, faced with the demolition of their homes, have sought to use the formal planning tools available and develop their own strategies to successfully stop or delay such plans. During the two and a half years of the research project that has led to this book, we have witnessed how many of the campaigns confronting the demolition of their neighbourhoods were successful in stopping, or in some cases delaying at crucial junctures, the projects that would have led to the loss of their homes.

They have done this either through proposing alternative plans or by gaining decision-making power over the regeneration of their neighbourhood. In doing so, community groups have used a combination of formal planning tools and informal actions and strategies outside planning. The experience gained by campaigners in opposing the demolition of their homes, proposing alternative plans and gaining decision-making power can be very useful for others facing similar situations. This book has been put together in order to help such communities. It both presents these experiences and provides a toolkit of planning and design tools, along with informal actions on the margins of planning, that other communities can use to oppose the demolition of their neighbourhoods and to develop community-led plans.

The structure of the book builds on previous work by scholars and activists, especially the collaborative work of London Tenants Federation, Loretta Lees, Just Space and Southwark Notes Archive Group in *Staying Put: An Anti-Gentrification Handbook for Council Estates in London*.[1] This is part of a long tradition of recording on paper the experiences of urban struggles against demolition and regeneration in London, including most notably *The Battle for Tolmers Square* by Nick Wates[2] and the chronicle of the battles against demolition in the Covent Garden area in the late 1970s.[3] International examples include *Displacement: How to Fight It* by Hartmann, Keating and LeGates[4] and *Towards the City of Thresholds* by Stavros Stavrides.[5] These chronicles and handbooks form part of a wider critique of top–bottom mainstream planning and the development of a 'planning from below'.[6]

There is a diversity of contemporary international initiatives adopted by communities faced with demolition of their homes, as they use or develop new tools and strategies. Some examples, which can be contextual international references, include Beirut Public Works Studio's *Think Housing* project from 2019,[7] Boston's City Life / Vida Urbana *Sword and Shield* action in support of the Just Cause Eviction law,[8] Milan's *Isola Art Centre* planning projects to counter the demolition of a housing complex[9] and Barcelona's *Repensar Bonpastor* community-led competition of ideas, promoted by the International Alliance of Inhabitants.[10]

Taking into account both local and international cases of community-led challenges to regeneration projects, we can see that this book is timely. Around the world interest in community planning has markedly increased in the last decade, in particular, as a response to austerity politics and the effects of neoliberal urban developments on communities. This is reflected in the UK, especially in the role that some communities are having within estate regeneration, but also in the specifics of London's housing struggles.

Some housing or planning policy will no doubt change over time, but unfortunately it is unlikely that pressures on social housing will disappear in London any time soon. We consider therefore that the case study material will remain useful for some years to come. Even as material from campaigns, including for better housing, and community-led planning from the 1970s and 1980s is still relevant today, so the stories and experiences featured here will continue to point towards alternative housing futures.

The first part of the book includes seven case studies of communities self-organising to have stronger decision-making power over their neighbourhoods. Many of these have resisted demolition proposals and proposed alternative approaches. Building both on the lessons learned from these case studies and from a review of the existing planning tools, schemes, policies and other strategies, the second part of the book offers a toolkit for communities and planners engaged in developing community-led regeneration plans.

How we have written this book

In collaboration with community groups

This research project has been developed in collaboration with Just Space, a London-wide alliance of community groups, with the aim of producing outputs useful for community groups. The research process has included the co-organisation of seminars and workshops (fig.0.1) with Just Space and participation in other community events. One of the aims of organising these workshops is the establishing of communities' priorities; the research has been framed with this in mind. The workshops also sought to stimulate further collaboration between researchers and community organisations. Each of the seven case studies included semi-structured interviews involving residents and other people or organisations supporting the community groups, as well as community groups' own participation in the workshops held. Since Just Space is an 'informal alliance' of community groups,[11] only some of the groups discussed in this book, such as Greater Carpenters Neighbourhood Forum, might identify themselves specifically as members; others are not necessarily members of Just Space, although they attend events of the network and feel supported by it. This book therefore builds on the knowledge generated by these campaigns, community organisations and people who support them. It is important to recognise their contribution to knowledge, which is useful for other campaigns, and also to acknowledge their help in putting this book together.

While the research project has not collaborated directly with the seven case studies, since these represent situations where ongoing campaigns have already used the planning tools discussed in this book, it has produced outcomes that can assist other community organisations, as noted below:

1. Contribution to consultation on the Mayor of London's strategic policy documents. We have supported Just Space in producing the responses for the Draft London Housing Strategy, as well as the consultation on the Greater London Authority's (GLA's) Resident Ballot Funding Condition. In addition to this, we also participated in the event organised by Just Space and the GLA at City Hall on the consultation on the draft London Plan. The outputs of these collaborations can be consulted on the website http://communityled.london:
   a. Sendra and Fitzpatrick's response to the Mayor of London's consultation on Resident ballots in estate regeneration – April 2018.[12]
   b. Contribution to Just Space's response to the Mayor of London's consultation on Resident ballots in estate regeneration – April 2018.[13]
   c. Contribution to Just Space's response to the Mayor of London's Draft Housing Strategy on the issues related to estate regeneration – December 2017.[14]
2. The publication of a toolkit for residents and planners (this book) to support residents seeking to oppose social housing demolition and propose community-led plans. The publication of this book in open access by UCL Press allows residents and planners to download it for free.
3. Although this project has not directly collaborated with a group of residents in opposing demolition and proposing alternatives, the experience gained in working on this project has helped one of the authors to collaborate with a group of residents on South Kilburn Estate in opposing demolition and proposing alternatives. Through the Civic Design CPD course at The Bartlett School of Planning, Pablo Sendra worked both with the students taking the course and with Granville Community Kitchen to produce evidence on the impact of demolition and to prepare a first draft of a community plan for refurbishment and infill around two of the towers of the estate.[15] This collaboration for drafting a community plan is continuing now through a knowledge exchange project titled 'Civic Design Exchange: Co-Designing Neighbourhoods with Residents', funded by the Higher Education Innovation Fund, Research England.

Figure 0.1 Workshop on 'Community-Led Estate Regeneration', held as part of the Just Space conference organised for consultation on the Draft London Housing Strategy. November 2017. Image: Pablo Sendra.

Analysis of tools, strategies and actors in seven case studies

The seven case studies presented here are: a) Walterton and Elgin Community Homes (WECH), b) West Ken Gibbs Green Community Homes (WKGGCH), c) Cressingham Gardens Community, d) Greater Carpenters Neighbourhood Forum (GCNF), e) Focus E15, f) People's Empowerment Alliance for Custom House (PEACH) and g) Alexandra and Ainsworth Estates. The communities in these case studies have used different strategies: direct action, occupation, legal action, neighbourhood planning, People's Plans co-design workshops and fundraising. The analysis of the case studies has consisted of semi-structured interviews with residents, community organisers, campaigners, volunteers, architects working for those communities, and other people and organisations supporting those communities. The research has focused on the strategies that communities have used (both inside and outside formal planning frameworks), and on the interaction between the different actors involved.

In four of the case studies (WKGGCH, Cressingham Gardens Community, GCNF and Focus E15), diagrams have been used to explain the combination of tools, strategies and actions used by the community group, as well as the actors involved. These diagrams were produced for a paper that grew from this same research project. It uses assemblage theory to explain the complexity of the combination of tools and actors in opposing demolition and proposing alternative plans.[16] The diagrams are shown in this book because they illustrate well the diversity of tools and actors in each case study.

Review of planning tools for community-led regeneration

In producing this toolkit, in addition to exploring the case studies, we have reviewed the available planning frameworks, regulations and policies that provide residents with control, ownership and decision-making powers, or simply allow them to participate. We have then organised these tools into five chapters: a) 'Gaining residents' control', b) 'Localism Act 2011', c) 'Policies for community participation in regeneration', d) 'Using the law and challenging redevelopment through the courts' and e) 'Informal tools and strategies'. For each of the tools, we have explained its use for communities proposing their own regeneration plan, the difficulties such communities may encounter and how to overcome them, the situations recommended for each tool's use and the technical and financial support available. We have also identified the case studies using the tool.

How to use this toolkit

This toolkit is designed for communities resisting the demolition of their homes and/or proposing their own alternative plan, and for planners, architects, professionals, scholars and volunteers providing support to those community groups. As noted, the case studies presented in this book are all located in London, and some of the policies in chapter 10 apply specifically to the capital. However, this toolkit is by no means limited to people and campaigns based in London. Most of the tools presented here also apply to similar situations throughout England and Wales.

Furthermore, the toolkit is also useful for communities and planners outside the UK; its purpose is not just to explain particular planning regulations and frameworks, but also to discuss the strategies that other case studies have followed. These strategies include the combination of formal and informal planning tools, establishing alliances and getting support from other organisations, and seeking support from professionals to help with their campaign and community-led plan.[17] In addition to this, informal tools such as putting together a People's Plan or other campaigning strategies are applicable in other contexts; they do not relate to any particular policy.

While planning frameworks and regulations may change over time, there is much to learn from the case studies. We show how they have used a combination of tools, and in what sequence, and reveal the alliances created during the process. The book constantly cross-references case studies and tools, believing that readers will gain most by both examining the toolkit itself and discovering how different case studies have used it in combination with other tools.

Notes

1. London Tenants Federation, Loretta Lees, Just Space and Southwark Notes Archive Group. 2014. *Staying Put: An Anti-Gentrification Handbook for Council Estates in London*. London: Just Space. https://justspacelondon.files.wordpress.com/2014/06/staying-put-web-version-low. pdf. Accessed 1 August 2019.
2. Nick Wates. 1976 [2013]. *The Battle for Tolmers Square*. London: Routledge Revivals.
3. Brian Anson. 1981. *I'll Fight You For It! Behind the Struggle for Covent Garden, 1966–74*. London: Jonathan Cape.
4. Chester Hartmann, Dennis Keating and Richard LeGates, with Steve Turner. 1982. *Displacement: How to Fight It*. San Francisco: National Housing Law Project.
5. Stavros Stavrides. 2018. *Towards the City of Thresholds*. New York: Common Notions.
6. In particular it is worth looking at the work of Libby Porter, including *Unlearning the Colonial Cultures of Planning* from 2009 and the 2010 Right to the City Alliance report on public housing, 'We Call These Projects Home', https://righttothecity.org/cause/we-call-these-projects-home. Accessed 1 August 2019.
7. Public Works Studio. 'About Us'. https://publicworksstudio.com/en/about. Accessed 1 August 2019.
8. City Life / Vida Urbana. http://www.clvu.org. Accessed 1 August 2019.
9. Isola Art Centre. http://isolartcenter.org/en/chi-siamo/. Accessed 23 January 2020.
10. Repensar Bonpastor. https://repensarbonpastor.wordpress.com. Accessed 1 August 2019.
11. Just Space. n.d. 'About Just Space'. https://justspace.org.uk/about/. Accessed 31 July 2019.
12. Pablo Sendra and Daniel Fitzpatrick. 2018. 'Response to the Consultation Paper "Proposed New Funding Condition to Require Resident Ballots in Estate Regeneration"'. Community-Led Social Housing Regeneration (9 April 2018). http://communityled.london/wp-content/uploads/2018/04/Response-to-ballot-consultation-PS-and-DF-UCL.pdf. Accessed 31 July 2019.
13. Just Space. 2018. 'Estate Ballots'. https://justspace.org.uk/2018/04/13/estate-ballots/. Accessed 31 July 2019.
14. Just Space. 2013. 'Housing: Not Good Enough'. https://justspace.org.uk/2017/12/07/housing-not-good-enough. Accessed 31 July 2019.
15. The Bartlett School of Planning, UCL. 2019. 'CPD Civic Design'. https://www.ucl.ac.uk/bartlett/planning/programmes/cpd-civic-design. Accessed 31 July 2019.
16. Pablo Sendra. 2018. 'Assemblages for Community-Led Social Housing Regeneration: Activism, Big Society and Localism', *City* 22(5–6): 738–62.
17. Pablo Sendra. 2018. 'Assemblages for Community-Led Social Housing Regeneration: Activism, Big Society and Localism'.

Part I
Case Studies

This first part of the book presents seven case studies of residents and campaigns that have challenged the demolition of social housing estates in London and/or proposed community-led plans. We have selected seven case studies that use a variety of tools, so people who use this toolkit have access to a range of options depending on their situation.

The campaigns selected had different objectives. Greater Carpenters Neighbourhood Forum, Cressingham Gardens Community and West Ken Gibbs Green Community Homes are fighting against the demolition of their homes and suggesting alternative, community-led plans. The People's Empowerment Alliance for Custom House is not opposing the demolition, but they are proposing a community-led plan and have managed to get the council to treat them as partners in the regeneration process. Focus E15 is a group of women, mostly single mothers, who when faced with eviction decided to form a campaign group for proper rehousing. They are not a group of housing estate residents opposing the demolition of their neighbourhood, but they did, through their campaign, end up campaigning against the demolition of the Carpenters Estate and provided support to other housing campaigns. Walterton and Elgin Community Homes no longer needs to fight against the demolition of their homes because the community owns the estates. They mounted a strong and successful campaign in the late 1980s and early 1990s that led to the transfer of the housing stock from the council to a community-owned housing association. Alexandra and Ainsworth Estates does not need to fight against demolition either because Alexandra Road buildings were Grade II* listed in 1993. The residents have been successful in getting funding from the Heritage Lottery Fund to refurbish their park, however, providing a great example of community-led regeneration. They are now facing some problems with the repairs, maintenance and heating system of the estate.

This diversity of campaigns provides a set of tools and strategies for people who wish to use this toolkit. The case studies cross-reference the tools explained in more detail in the second part of this book. It is important in using this toolkit to look both at the tools themselves and at the cases that have employed them.

1

Walterton and Elgin Community Homes

Walterton and Elgin Community Homes (WECH) is a resident-controlled, community-owned housing organisation in north Paddington.[1] It emerged out of a long-running campaign during the 1980s to prevent the sale and demolition by Westminster City Council of two large estates. WECH was able to use the so-called Tenants' Choice legislation in the 1988 Housing Act to take over the management and ownership of 921 homes from the local authority, and is now one of the largest Community Land Trusts in England and Wales.[2]

The housing north of Harrow Road in north Paddington had been built between 1865 and 1885. The land was bought in 1953 by the London County Council (LCC), which waited for the leases to expire in 1964. In the meantime the properties became used by speculative landlords who crammed the properties with tenants, charging high rents and undertaking few repairs. They left the housing in poor condition, typical of Rachmanite slum landlordism.[3] In 1964 the area returned to the LCC, which became the Greater London Council (GLC) the following year. The authority divided the area into four strategic zones, slowly beginning the demolition, rehabilitation and sale of properties.

By 1980 the remaining GLC properties were concentrated on the Walterton and the Elgin estates. These were transferred to Westminster Council, which proposed selling the estates off to private developers for a dense rebuild programme. In a very swift response to this, residents formed the Walterton and Elgin Action Group (WEAG), demanding that the council withdraw its plans and prioritise residents' needs and wishes (fig.1.1). Eventually WEAG drew up its own plan for the provision of better homes for local people. The campaign persisted, and for the next three years the group lobbied the council's Housing Committee, with over 100 people regularly attending its meetings.

We are a little worried
about our landlord.

Figure 1.1 A poster designed by John Phillips for Walterton and Elgin Action Group, 1985. It was used to adorn the hoardings on empty houses and as part of a communications campaign with Westminster Council. Image: John Phillips.

Despite this campaign, the council's committee pushed forward with a variety of schemes including a 'barter deal' with developers for the Walterton and Elgin estates. Under this proposal, the developers would receive half of the properties built to sell on the open market in exchange for the refurbishment of the other half for council tenants.

In the 1988 Housing Act the Tenants' Choice provision was introduced, which WEAG used to take over the control of the council properties. Approval as a landlord was needed from the Housing Corporation. A ballot of residents was held, and the Action Group formed Walterton and Elgin Community Homes (WECH) with advice from local housing association Paddington Churches Housing Association (PCHA). A committee elected by residents was set up, which included housing, finance and management professionals. In March 1989, with three-quarters of residents signed up, WECH became the first approved landlord under the 1988 Housing Act legislation to submit their application.

During this period WECH solidified its support among residents through meetings and visits with residents to explain and gather residents' concerns. Because of this outreach work a manifesto was published in September 1991 outlining the options of staying with the council or transferring to WECH. Of the 82 per cent of residents who participated in the ballot, 72 per cent were in favour of transfer. This duly took place in April 1992 and between 1993 and 1997 Westminster Council paid over £22 million to WECH. WECH implemented a high-quality building and refurbishment programme'.[4] WECH also got £3.5 million from the Housing Corporation and in addition put a loan facility in place.

Once the first transfer occurred, the hard work of refurbishment began. Phase 1 focused on Walterton estate, where works were undertaken on around 212 Victorian terraced houses at an average cost of £72,000 per house. Funding was provided partly by WECH and partly through a housing allocation grant (HAG). Throughout 1992 consultations continued with residents to discuss scope of works, residents' concerns and the choices available. WECH's architects developed a design brief for the whole estate with standardised conversions, which could be adapted in response to residents' needs and wishes. The process of moving house within the estate was negotiated carefully to meet residents' wishes, with WECH honouring its commitment that no one would be forced to move against their will.

The whole refurbishment process was carried out in batches of two to five houses, with a total of 30 contracts made in under five years. Competitive tendering was used throughout and the architect was able to control costs as experience with the process grew. A national recession also resulted in lower building costs, and the unit cost remained roughly the same throughout the refurbishment programme. Residents who had bought their properties under Right to Buy arrangements could swap their home for a new one of the same size. A total of 25 swaps were made. Many of those involved were people who would never otherwise have been able to improve their homes and remain in the area.

WECH was also able to help the council with homeless people in the borough who needed temporary accommodation. They initially provided housing for 73 homeless households. Subsequently, in a second deal, 39 flats were provided for three years, and by 1997 a third leasing scheme involving 25 flats for four years was arranged. Short-life housing organisations also continue to license property from WECH, which provides two nominations per year for permanent housing to short-life residents.

Health improvements were also notable in this period, especially in conditions related to stress.[5] Residents felt empowered through their involvement, and this complemented the provision of high-quality housing and an improved sense of community among residents.[6] The refurbishment was also noted for its conservation-based approach, even though the Victorian properties were not listed nor in a conservation area.

Phase 2 of refurbishment focused on Athens and Kincardine Gardens in the middle of Elgin estate and comprising 96 homes in eight blocks of between two and four storeys. The cost per home was £46,916 and WECH sourced all the funding required. The walkways between blocks were demolished, individual stair towers were provided, and pitched roofs and external cladding for thermal insulation were added. New communal facilities included central heating and the redesign of public areas. Resident participation was again crucial; meetings were held and each resident was able to make choices concerning kitchen units and layouts, bathroom preferences and security. As part of this phase the community centre was expanded. Eventually the two asbestos-ridden high-rise blocks were demolished, making way for a third phase of building new homes.

In Phase 3, a total of 55 new homes were built between 1995 and 1997 for a cost of £53,660 per home. These replaced 202 tower block flats with a lower-density scheme: between two and three storeys in height, plus gardens and space for play. A further project was achieved through the sale of a small site owned by WECH to the North British Housing Association (NBHA); this was able to consolidate and create a larger site for social housing. In exchange, NBHA refurbished the adjoining three levels of garages in 1999.

An innovative scheme providing 43 new affordable rented homes on extra floors built over existing homes, new infill blocks, a new stand-alone building and conversions on one of its existing estates is nearing completion (fig.1.2). It took 15 years of consideration and iteration, numerous refinements and a great deal of financial preparation. The work has also been undertaken with residents in occupation. The project is built to high environmental standards, providing passive ventilation,[7] 140 KW of solar power with batteries, green roofs and living walls.

The scheme is financed by means of a £9m loan and a £1m grant from WECH, £4m from the council's S106 monies, £2.6m from the Mayor of London and £0.4m from the Government's Community Housing Fund.[8] In return for the grant, WECH has agreed to provide 80 per cent of new lettings for council nominations, retaining 20 per cent in perpetuity to meet its own population's needs. This scheme provides, entirely at the community landlord's expense, a new community centre that can be used by three groups at once, a provision for other organisations supplying community services, new office facilities and purpose-built pre-school facilities, open to families from the wider area. The scheme should be completed by March 2020.

Tools used

During the initial stages of the Walterton and Elgin Action Group (WEAG) campaign, residents would attend the council's Housing Committee regularly and visit the developers who indicated potential interest in the council's scheme. This tactic involved residents who, in activist mode, made impromptu visits to the developer's offices, accompanied by musicians, posters (see fig.1.1) and placards, to argue their case with management. By 1988 this organised campaign had reduced the number of developers interested in the scheme to only one.

Once established as WECH, residents were able to use a piece of legislation in the 1988 Housing Act to take over the management and ownership of the houses that had been designated for sale. The so-called Tenants' Choice legislation, introduced by the Conservative government in 1988, was repealed in 1996, however, following only a handful of transfers, of which the most significant was WECH. Despite repealing the law, the principle has subsequently been adopted with the Right to Transfer (see chapter 8), the Regulations for which were made in November 2013. However, it remains to be fully tested.

As WECH is now in full community control, it has been able to develop its own regeneration programme, effectively implementing its own form of People's Plan (see chapter 12). The existing community centre and office are being converted to homes, and new homes are being added on an extra floor above existing blocks, as described above, with new community facilities to be completed by March 2020 (fig.1.2).

Figure 1.2   New social housing under construction in Walterton and Elgin Community Homes. January 2018. Image: Pablo Sendra.

Current and future challenges

Throughout WECH's lifetime, efforts have been made to increase residents' involvement, developing their capacity as well as their loyalty. Around three-quarters of WECH tenants and leaseholders are members of WECH, who elect the Board at an AGM once a year. The Board has 14 residents and six external professionals, reflecting both WECH's population as well as its needs to have housing and financial expertise on their Board. In addition, several committees meet to run particular activities within WECH.

The WECH AGM is crucial to maximise Board accountability to the residents and WECH has worked hard to maintain high levels of attendance. In addition, another strength of the community-led housing approach is WECH's strong awareness of its impact on the local economy. In 1997 WECH organised a conference on social housing developments in the area, which stimulated a broader discussion about the local economy. WECH owns the freehold of four shops on the Walterton estate and has set aside a budget to help with community regeneration activities.

In addition, WECH supports the local economy by having its own fair rental system: 2016 rents have been increased by 0.9 per cent, equivalent to 1 per cent below the year-on-year increase in the Consumer Price Index recorded for September 2015. This increase is well below market level, and lower than most council and housing association rents in the area.[9] In 1998 WECH decided to have a unified staff structure, taking management and maintenance services in house. Soon after, it also took finance and then development in house.

Studies have been conducted over the last decade to evaluate the impacts of resident control. One study concluded that, despite high levels of deprivation, WECH residents were happier and more engaged under community ownership than under their previous council landlord.[10] They feel a stronger sense of belonging to their neighbourhood than the national average, and are more satisfied with their homes and with their landlord than council tenants across London. They also declare a higher degree of active participation.

WECH continues to provide a campaigning exemplar as well as influencing community-led housing policy. The challenges are in the translation of these policies into practices by other groups who may be operating in different contexts to those faced by WECH. For example, the process of translating and communicating WECH's successes into policy measures at national, London and local authority levels has become part of its current ongoing activity.

Key lessons

- Use of direct action to raise awareness, targeting key actors and institutions.
- Involvement of residents in the political processes locally, including Housing and Planning Committees and other decision-making bodies in local authorities and beyond.
- Establishment of a core group of members as well as support beyond the group and local area through communications, information and involvement.
- Use of legislation at local and national levels to increase control over maintenance, management and even ownership of homes by groups of residents.
- There are measurable benefits associated with empowerment through community ownership, which appear to mitigate the detriment to well-being caused by financial deprivation, physical illness and fear of crime.[11]
- Residents perceive WECH as an organisation that 'listens' to their concerns and 'cares' about them, their homes and the neighbourhood. Most commonly, they say that WECH has 'helped' them individually and as a community.
- The key principles of WECH which can be taken from its history include the form of community ownership, resident control and neighbourhood-based organisation that enables WECH to contribute to community cohesion and engage in various and neighbourhood initiatives. These in turn lead to real and perceived improvements in a wide range of aspects of people's lives such as health, safety, employment and mental wellbeing.
- WECH has estate-based staff who can respond to the needs of residents and ensure the homes and the neighbourhood are well maintained.
- Lower rents than the local average for social and housing association properties allow residents to be less reliant on benefits. They are able to manage an acceptable lifestyle even when in low-paid jobs, to save for future needs and to provide support for family members.
- Community ownership allows WECH to preserve housing stock for future generations. The transfer of properties thus allows social housing to be preserved in perpetuity.
- An interesting side point is that WECH has a Police in Residence scheme, providing a home for a local police officer at an affordable rent. The officer is involved in local community activities, including the Bike Auction and WECH Community Services. They also serve as a point of liaison with local police and safety services and help to raise awareness on community safety.[12]

Notes

1. We would like to acknowledge the invaluable contribution to this chapter made by Jonathan Rosenberg, campaigner, community organiser and current chair of WECH.
2. See WECH. 1999. *Against the Odds: Walterton and Elgin from Campaign to Control.* London: WECH.
3. Rachman was a slum landlord in West London during the 1950s. He was notorious for exploiting his tenants in properties that were overcrowded and under-maintained.
4. WECH. n.d. 'How We Started'. http://wech.co.uk/company-who-we-are/about-us-who-we-are-what-we-do-etc/how-we-started.html. Accessed 18 November 2019.
5. Peter Ambrose and Julia Stone conducted in-depth interviews with 26 per cent of WECH's 600 tenants and leaseholders between February and July 2010. See Peter Ambrose and Julia Stone. 2010. *Happiness, Heaven and Hell in Paddington: A Comparative Study of the Empowering Management Practices of WECH.* Brighton: University of Sussex.
6. Madhu Satsangi and Susan Murray. 2011. *Community Empowerment. Final Report to Walterton and Elgin Community Homes.* Stirling: University of Stirling.
7. Natural ventilation without the use of mechanical systems.
8. From correspondence with Jonathan Rosenberg, 21 July 2019.
9. WECH. 2016. *Walterton & Elgin Community Homes Annual Report 2015/16.*
10. Jonathan Rosenberg. 2011. *Measuring the Benefits of Empowerment through Community Ownership: Summary of Evidence Gathered from the Population of a Mutual Resident-Controlled Housing Association and Compared at Various Levels.* Submission of evidence to DCLG to support the Right to Transfer, 2011.
11. Satsangi and Murray. 2011. *Community Empowerment.*
12. WECH. 2016. *Walterton & Elgin Community Homes Annual Report 2015/16.*

2
West Ken Gibbs Green Community Homes

West Kensington and Gibbs Green (WKGG) are two housing estates located in the London Borough of Hammersmith and Fulham, next to the piece of land where the Earl's Court Exhibition Centre used to be before its demolition (fig.2.1).[1] The estates are part of the Earl's Court and West Kensington Opportunity Area. The plans for redeveloping the estates form part of a large private development led by Capital & Counties Properties PLC (Capco), which encompasses the site across the Earl's Court area spread over two local authorities – the London Borough of Hammersmith and Fulham and the Royal Borough of Kensington and Chelsea. This large scheme is now in a critical situation.

The neighbours started to campaign against the council's plans to sell the land for redevelopment in 2009.[2] The local MP for Hammersmith and Fulham approached Jonathan Rosenberg, who in the late 1980s had succeeded both in stopping Westminster Council from selling the homes of Walterton and Elgin estates to developers and in completing the transfer of housing stock from Westminster Council to a community-owned housing association – Walterton and Elgin Community Homes – in 1992 (see chapter 1). Since Jonathan joined the residents of WKGG as community organiser, they have been using diverse strategies to stop the sale of the land and gain residents' control. After years of campaigning, the council has now declared its intention of stopping the sale of the land to private developers.

Tools used

One of the first moves of West Kensington and Gibbs Green residents after Rosenberg joined them as community organiser was to set up the Community

Figure 2.1   View of the estates from one of the flats. January 2017.
Image: Pablo Sendra.

Land Trust West Ken Gibbs Green Community Homes (WKGGCH), with the
aim of applying for a Right to Transfer (see chapter 8). This piece of legislation, an amendment to the 1985 Housing Act, was enacted in the Housing
and Regeneration Act 2008. It allows residents to gain collective ownership
and control of their homes and propose their own regeneration scheme, as
Walterton and Elgin residents had done through the 1988 Tenants' Choice
legislation. Since the Regulations for the Right to Transfer were not published
until November 2013, the residents could not give valid notice before this
date and were only able finally to give the Right to Transfer notice in August
2015.

In anticipation of having to carry out a feasibility study, WKGGCH
hired Architects for Social Housing (ASH) to translate their vision for new
homes and improvements into an architectural proposal for a People's
Plan (see chapter 12). This proposed building between 200 and 300 new
homes without demolishing any of the existing housing.[3] On 10 July 2019,
while finishing this book, the Ministry of Housing, Communities and Local
Government determined, on behalf of the Secretary of State, 'that the
stock transfer process in relation to WKGG estates should not continue'
on the grounds 'that WKGGCH's proposed transfer will have a significant

detrimental impact on the regeneration of the area'.[4] The determination also says that '(t)here is sufficient ground to conclude that the Earls Court regeneration scheme is making concrete progress'.[5] However, according to *Inside Housing*, after meeting with the Leader of the Council, the Mayor of London said that Capco '... has proved incapable of bringing anything forward ... . I have no confidence in the ability of Capco to manage a development of this scale and all options for breaking the current impasse must be considered – including the council exercising its ability to acquire the site using a compulsory purchase order'.[6] As one of the Board members of WKGGCH noted on Twitter,[7] the Mayor's statement contradicts the Ministry of Housing, Communities and Local Government's determination.

Despite having not yet achieved the transfer of stock from the local authority to a community-owned company, this is a good example of knowledge transfer from past experiences; it also serves as an example of testing a new piece of legislation. WKGGCH's ambition of gaining community ownership and control of their homes as a response to the threat of privatisation and demolition is inspired by WECH's success in the late 1980s and early 1990s. Campaigns learn from each other and also learn from past experiences: important pointers for this toolkit. Another group of residents in London, Cressingham Gardens (see chapter 3) in the London Borough of Lambeth, also served notice for the Right to Transfer. In this case, the Ministry of Housing, Communities and Local Government, on behalf of the Secretary of State, has determined that the transfer of the housing stock to Cressingham Gardens Community should continue[8] – a positive outcome to inspire other residents who want to pursue this route. This experience is also a useful test of whether this new piece of legislation works or not in granting residents the ownership and control of their homes. In this sense, Rosenberg has highlighted the problems of this new piece of legislation in comparison to the 1988 Tenants' Choice legislation used by WECH in the early 1990s.[9]

At the same time as the community was preparing to serve notice for the Right to Transfer, the council was continuing its plans to sell the land to the developer. This was challenged by means of a Judicial Review (see chapter 11) by the residents. Although this challenge was eventually dismissed, the judge praised the residents for the quality of their submission and emphasised their right to challenge the decision in the first place.[10] The Judicial Review did not manage to stop the Conditional Land Sale Agreement (CLSA), but it did delay it. In January 2013 the council signed a CLSA with the developer Capco. As the CLSA requires residents to be rehoused before any land is transferred,[11] all the estates remain in council ownership.

Despite being a long campaign, West Kensington and Gibbs Green's residents have stayed strong and unified for many years, gaining support from politicians, professionals, scholars, urban planning students and other activists. In January 2018, as a result of years of campaigning and the use of diverse strategies, planning tools and actions,[12] the council, which had changed from Conservative to Labour in 2014, demanded that the developers hand back the estate to the council.[13]

This was an important milestone in the residents' intention to avoid displacement. It was also an important achievement: one that can influence other councils and residents across London and provide a positive demonstration of the impact that collective action and campaigning can have. While writing this book, the authors attended a preview screening of the film that WKGGCH is making about the campaign, along with a series of other historical films on tenants and residents who took control of housing in other parts of the UK. The screening, held in the estate's community centre, was attended by many residents as well as people who had supported or sympathised with the campaign during its history. The atmosphere of the event was positive and buoyant. The final workshop of this research project on 11 June 2019 was also held in Gibbs Green Community Hall, where participants had the opportunity to share their experiences on proposing community-led regeneration.

WKGGCH has used a combination of formal and informal tools and strategies for opposing demolition and for proposing a community-led plan (see fig.2.2). These include demonstrations, letter writing, sending emails to developers, drafting a People's Plan and engaging with formal planning tools such as the Right to Transfer. Through this combination of strategies, they have developed a number of capabilities as a resident group. The first is the ability to run a long-lasting campaign – 10 years so far – and to fight a massive development and developer. When the community organiser and a resident were asked to identify their most effective strategy in the campaign, they responded that 'by far it is visiting people in their homes and maintaining close relations with individuals and households over time and building up trust'.[14] Bringing the community together has helped provide them with a clear vision and the strength to maintain a long-lasting campaign. This is having a knock-on effect on development opportunities for the area; in the press release for its 2015 annual report, the developer identified activist opposition as a risk.[15] This sustained campaigning has also contributed to the council's decision to claim back the estates from Capco.

WKGGCH has also had the capacity to raise funds to pay for staff and consultants. They have a housing organiser and a community organiser,

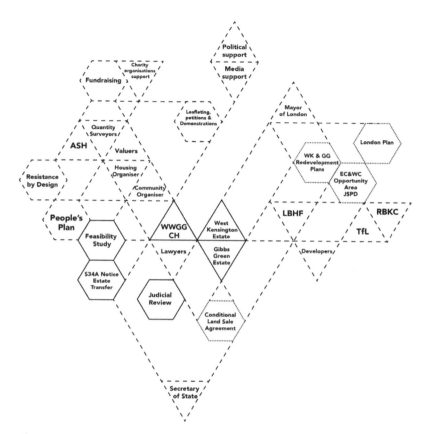

Figure 2.2 Assemblage of actors, actions, strategies, formal planning framework and policies in the context of West Kensington and Gibbs Green. Triangles represent the actors involved. A continuous line shows those directly involved; those with a dashed line are indirectly involved or supporting actors. Hexagons represent actions, strategies, formal planning tools and policies. Those with a continuous line are those that engage with formal planning. Those with a dashed line represent actions or strategies outside formal planning, while those with a dotted line are strategies developed by public authorities.[16] Created by Pablo Sendra.

and have also hired architects for a six-month period to draft the People's Plan, as well as valuers and surveyors. This support from experts and someone like Rosenberg with experience of community ownership has proved very important for the campaign.

Current and future challenges

The council now has the intention of stopping the sale of the land to the private developer. This cancellation of the CLSA is one of the main challenges. The recent determination of the Secretary of State that the Right to Transfer (RtT) should not continue raises a new challenge for residents, who will need to find ways to pursue their aspiration of community ownership.

Key lessons

- Lengthy campaigning and the use of a combination of formal planning tools, testing new pieces of legislation and other forms of informal planning and activism can be effective.
- Strong campaigns by community groups can make the acquisition of land or property less attractive to developers, as they often view such campaigns as a hurdle to their plans and introduce more risks into their costings.
- The presence of a community organiser with previous experience in similar campaigns is very helpful. Housing organisers and architects can also contribute to make the campaign stronger.
- Gaining the support of politicians, universities and other campaigns helps to make the campaign stronger.

Notes

1. This chapter builds on two previous publications, which were updated to January 2017 and May 2019. Since those publications, there have been changes that can be helpful for other residents working on similar strategies. This chapter is updated to July 2019. The two previous publications are: Pablo Sendra. 2018. 'Assemblages for Community-Led Social Housing Regeneration: Activism, Big Society and Localism', *City* 22(5–6): 738–62; Pablo Sendra and Daniel Fitzpatrick. 2020. 'Time to Be an Activist: Recent Successes in London Housing Activism', in *Critical Dialogues of Urban Governance, Development and Activism: London & Toronto*, Susannah Bunce, Nicola Livingstone, Susan Moore and Alan Walks, eds. London: UCL Press.
2. Interview with community organiser Jonathan Rosenberg and WKGG resident Harold Greatwood, January 2017.
3. Interview with Jonathan Rosenberg, community organiser of WKGGCH, and WKGG resident Harold Greatwood, 6 January 2017. Interview with Geraldine Dening, ASH, 26 January 2017. See also Architects for Social Housing. 2016. 'Feasibility Study Report: West Kensington and Gibbs Green Estates. New Homes and Improvements without Demolition'. https://architects-forsocialhousing.files.wordpress.com/2016/08/wkgg_report_rev3.pdf. Accessed 23 July 2019.
4. Ministry of Housing, Communities and Local Government. 2019. 'Right to Transfer Determinations: West Kensington and Gibbs Green Estates', 9 July 2019. https://assets.publishing. service.gov.uk/government/uploads/system/uploads/attachment_data/file/816103/West_ Ken_Gibbs_Green_determination_letter_Redacted.pdf. Accessed 16 July 2019.

5. Ministry of Housing, Communities and Local Government. 2019. 'Right to Transfer Determinations: West Kensington and Gibbs Green Estates', 9 July 2019.
6. Nathaniel Barker. 2019. 'Council Could Issue Order to Take Earl's Court Site from Developer, Claims Khan', *Inside Housing*, 19 July 2019. https://www.insidehousing.co.uk/news/news/council-could-issue-order-to-take-earls-court-site-from-developer-claims-khan-62364. Accessed 29 July 2019.
7. https://twitter.com/RobinHawkes1/status/1153214809057484800. Accessed 23 July 2019.
8. Ministry of Housing, Communities and Local Government. 2019. 'Right to Transfer Determinations: Cressingham Gardens Estate', 9 July 2019. https://assets.publishing.service.gov.uk/government/uploads/system/uploads/attachment_data/file/816102/Cressingham_Gardens_determination_letter_Redacted.pdf. Accessed 16 July 2019.
9. This emerged in the interviews with Jonathan Rosenberg in 2017 and from two reports he wrote on the legislation in 2012 and 2013.
10. Source: Jonathan Rosenberg, community organiser of WKGGCH, from the transcripts of the oral hearing on 23 April 2013 for reconsidering the previous judge's decision to refuse permission for Judicial Review. In this oral hearing the judge refused permission to Judicial Review. The judge also dismissed London Borough of Hammersmith and Fulham's application for costs.
11. London Borough of Hammersmith and Fulham. 2013. 'Conditional Land Sale Agreement in respect of the land of West Kensington and Gibbs Green Estates', 2013: 6. https://www.lbhf.gov.uk/sites/default/files/section_attachments/clsa_-_main_body.pdf. Accessed 23 July 2019.
12. Pablo Sendra. 2018. 'Assemblages for Community-Led Social Housing Regeneration: Activism, Big Society and Localism'.
13. Luke Barratt. 2019. 'Council Demands Return of Earls Court Estates', *Inside Housing*, 18 January 2018). https://www.insidehousing.co.uk/news/news/council-demands-return-of-earls-court-estates-54087. Accessed 23 July 2019.
14. Interview with community organiser Jonathan Rosenberg and WKGG resident Harold Greatwood, January 2017.
15. Capco's *Annual Report 2015* states: 'Due to its scale, there will remain a risk of protests or legal challenges (ranging from complaints about noise through to judicial reviews or applications for listing) against specific aspects of the scheme as it is progressed ... all such challenges to date have been successfully defended however future challenges of this nature cannot be discounted', Capital & Counties Properties PLC. *Annual Report & Accounts 2015*. http://www.annualreports.com/HostedData/AnnualReportArchive/C/LSE_CAPC_2015.pdf. Accessed 29 July 2019.
16. Pablo Sendra. 2018. 'Assemblages for Community-Led Social Housing Regeneration: Activism, Big Society and Localism'.

3
Cressingham Gardens Community

Cressingham Gardens is a council estate in Lambeth, South London.[1] Located near Brockwell Park, this low-rise medium-/high-density estate (fig.3.1) was built between 1967 and 1979. It was designed by a team of Lambeth architects led by Edward Hollamby.[2]

The Save Cressingham campaign started in September 2012, when an exhibition on the future of the estate raised suspicions among residents concerning the council's demolition plans. A group of residents quickly set up a Facebook page and designed leaflets with 'STOP DEMOLITION' written on them to make other residents aware of the situation. One of the first proposals that residents made to the council, in early 2013, was to follow a 'project plan' where they could have a 'common understanding of facts' – especially regarding the structural damage and the high cost of refurbishment alleged by the council without providing any evidence – in order to make informed decisions based on these facts.[3] In 2013 the council hired the company Social Life to run a 'consultation and co-production process';[4] the same company ran workshops with residents in late 2014.

The workshops and discussions within the 'project team'[5] between residents and the council from late 2014 to early 2015 considered five options, ranging from full refurbishment to full demolition, and their financial implications. In March 2015 the council made a cabinet[6] decision to reject the three options that considered refurbishment and to consider only the options that proposed partial or total redevelopment. Later, in July 2015, the council decided to fully redevelop the estate.

Tools used

Cressingham Gardens residents have used a combination of informal strategies and formal tools (see fig.3.3). These include campaigning, demonstrations, leafleting, actions to raise the awareness of other residents, putting together a

Figure 3.1 Residents and visitors walk around Cressingham Gardens during a theatrical performance representing community resistance to demolition. June 2016. Image: Pablo Sendra.

People's Plan (see chapter 12) with the support of an architect (fig. 3.2), twice bringing the council to Judicial Review (see chapter 11), serving notice for the Right to Transfer and Right to Manage (see chapter 8) (succeeding in both) and registering Assets of Community Value according to the Localism Act 2011 (see chapter 9).

After Lambeth Council decided at cabinet to reject the refurbishment options in March 2015, the residents brought this decision to Judicial Review. They claimed that the consultation had not been lawful as the council's cabinet had not taken residents' views into account and had decided not to proceed with the three refurbishment options, deeming them 'not affordable'.[7] The verdict was favourable to the residents' case and, in late 2015, the judge concluded that the decision of March 2015 had been 'unlawful' and 'quashed' it.[8]

After this first Judicial Review, the residents engaged a local architect and former resident of the estate, together with a local quantity surveyor, to help them put together the 'People's Plan'. This represented a community-led regeneration plan recording the demands of the community and providing up to 37 additional new homes, community spaces and workspaces mainly by transforming existing garage spaces (fig.3.2).[9] They ran a resident-led consultation process in early 2016, at the same time as a further council-organised consultation. The residents submitted the People's Plan to the council on 4 March 2016.[10] On 11 March officers from the Housing Regeneration Team produced a report which was to be

Figure 3.2 Architect's drawing of Cressingham Gardens' People's Plan, showing the additional homes in the garage spaces. Creator of the image: Ashvin De Vos, Variant Office, developed for Cressingham Gardens residents.

considered by the council's cabinet on 21 March. This report concluded that the People's Plan 'was not a viable proposition, technically very difficult and costly to achieve'.[11] Consequently the cabinet again decided to redevelop the estate and again residents brought this decision to Judicial Review. This time their claim was dismissed.[12]

In addition to the residents taking the council twice to Judicial Review (2015 and 2016) and producing a People's Plan, they have also used a wide range of formal and informal strategies and legal actions. They describe this strategy as 'cumulative',[13] using almost every planning framework, legal strategy and informal action or process available in order to propose a community-led plan that prevents demolition of the estate. Fig.3.3 shows the diversity of tools and strategies that residents have used. These include the Localism Act 2011 to register the community centre as an Asset of Community Value (see chapter 9) and applying for legal aid (see chapter 11) to bring the cabinet decisions of March 2015 and March 2016 to Judicial Review (see chapter 11). This cumulative strategy has created a strong campaign and increased the chances of success. Indeed, at the time of writing, the residents have succeeded in obtaining approval for both the Right to Manage and the Right to Transfer (see chapter 8) from central government.

The transfer of responsibility for the management of repairs on the estate from the council to a community-owned company, a Resident Management Organisation, has already taken place, and this company is now managing repairs up to a certain cost threshold. Cressingham Gardens residents had suffered for years from the poor repair and maintenance services provided by the council, causing the dilapidation of some of the homes and the frustration of residents who did not receive an appropriate

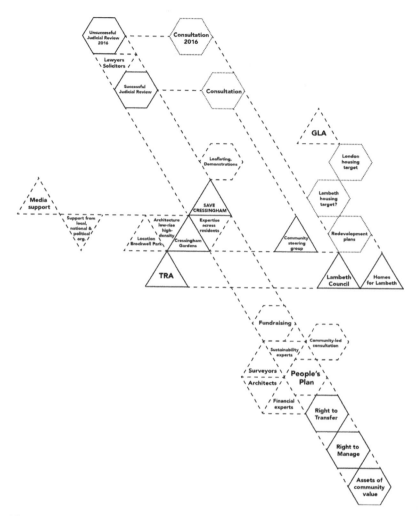

Figure 3.3 Assemblage of actors, actions, strategies, formal planning framework and policies in the context of Cressingham Gardens. Triangles represent the actors involved. Those with a continuous line are directly involved; those with a dashed line are indirectly involved or supporting actors. Hexagons represent actions, strategies, formal planning tools and policies. A continuous line shows those that engage with formal planning. A dashed line represents actions or strategies outside formal planning, while a dotted line shows strategies developed by public authorities.[14] Author: Pablo Sendra.

response or action from the council when repairs were required. After giving notice for the Right to Manage, Cressingham Gardens secured a legal ballot to transfer the management of repairs and maintenance from the council to a community-owned company. The ballot took place in November 2018, with 82.5 per cent of tenants voting in favour (77.9 per cent of secure tenants).[15] As a result of applying for the Right to Manage, the residents have had access both to central government funding and to technical support. They have also had support from the National Federation of Tenant Management Organisations. This organisation recommended to them a lawyer whose professional fees were covered by the local authority. Once the Resident Management Organisation is in place, they receive an allowance drawn from the Housing Revenue Account (HRA) of Lambeth Council to manage repairs and maintenance.[16]

More than three years after Cressingham Gardens residents gave notice to the London Borough of Lambeth (25 April 2016) for the Right to Transfer, the Ministry of Housing, Communities and Local Government, on behalf of the Secretary of State, determined 'that the stock transfer process in relation to the CGC (Cressingham Garden Community) should continue'. On 12 September 2016 Lambeth Council had asked the Secretary of State 'whether the proposed transfer of houses would have a significant detrimental effect on the regeneration of the area'. However, the Ministry of Housing, Communities and Local Government determined that the transfer 'will not have a significant detrimental effect on the provision of housing services, or the regeneration of the area'.[17]

It is clear from reading the determination that having a People's Plan that is both viable and well-supported by evidence is crucial. From this we see the importance of combining formal tools, like the Right to Transfer, with strategies that are not necessarily formal planning mechanisms, such as the People's Plan, which is not a statutory document. The People's Plan has been highly effective in bringing together the demands from residents and proposing alternative futures in very limited time frames. The residents carried out a consultation process which collected around 100 responses (from a total of 306 households), together with other surveys that had been carried out earlier.[18] The resultant People's Plan is a highly detailed, 326-page document. It includes 14 appendices containing reports on topics such as heritage conservation, the implementation of renewable energies and financial viability. This document demonstrates residents' ability to put together a community-led plan, with the support of professionals and backed with evidence and reports from experts. This would not have been achieved so quickly through a Neighbourhood Plan.

One characteristic of this campaign is the expertise that residents have developed during this process. Cressingham Gardens has a resident community with diverse skills; it has been able to react promptly, contest demolition and propose alternatives. The threat of losing their homes prompted many of them to use most of their free time to fight for their cause, providing a vast amount of unpaid labour and mutual support, and also building strong ties between residents.[19] This wholehearted commitment to the campaign and the use of a wide range of formal and informal strategies and legal actions has created great expertise in community-led planning and political activism. The campaign has used both in-house skills and external support and consultancies: voluntary or discounted work from professionals, legal aid lawyers and architects and other consultants paid through fundraising.

Another characteristic of this campaign has been its ability to operate through different kinds of formal and informal organisations, independent from one another, in order to engage with formal planning processes while also carrying out a housing campaign with no legal organisation. The initial discussions with the council were conducted through the Tenants and Residents Association (TRA). A project team was set up by the council and residents were included in it to discuss the regeneration options. The Judicial Reviews were carried out through individual claimants, although speaking on behalf of the whole community. In parallel to this, Save Cressingham acts as a housing campaign, with no legal organisation and no formal membership – a feature that contributes to flexibility and rapid action. For the Right to Manage and the Right to Transfer, the residents have set up a Resident Management Organisation (RMO). That organisation will then ramp up its activities into becoming the organisation that will take control of their homes.

Current/future challenges

Cressingham Gardens residents provide a very good example of strong and sustained campaigning. After years of work and effort, they have managed to be successful in both the Right to Manage and the Right to Transfer, which is unprecedented with these two pieces of legislation.

Earlier in 2018, when the Mayor of London launched a consultation on the Resident Ballot Condition for GLA Funding (see chapter 10), Cressingham Gardens residents discovered (from a response to a Freedom of Information (FOI) request)[20] that their estate was one of the exceptions and will not be balloted, since the GLA had already granted funding in December 2017 (just two months before the consultation was launched). While this decision has created some uncertainty among the residents, having been successful in the Right to Transfer they will have control to decide on the regeneration on their neighbourhood and their homes will be saved.

However, the transfer of stock has not yet been carried out. The residents now need to vote, by means of a ballot, to confirm the stock transfer and then also to develop a business plan. The case of Cressingham Gardens will be a good example to follow for residents who want to pursue this route.

Key lessons

- Campaigning and using a diverse set of planning tools, legal processes and other informal strategies makes the campaign strong.
- Using a mix of formal organisations and informal campaigning gives flexibility to adopt different strategies.
- Obtaining professional support and building in-house expertise make campaigns stronger.
- Right to Manage is a good tool to gain control of repairs and maintenance when the local authority is delivering a poor service. There is funding available for requesting it and setting up the management organisation. Once it is made effective, the management organisation receives an allowance from the council to manage repairs and maintenance.
- The Right to Transfer is a long process: it took three years to get approval from the Secretary of State, probably because it was one of the first cases under this piece of legislation. However, once it is made effective, residents will have full control over the regeneration of their estate. This is the most effective tool to secure the homes.

Notes

1. This chapter builds on a previous paper (Pablo Sendra. 2018. 'Assemblages for Community-Led Social Housing Regeneration: Activism, Big Society and Localism', *City* 22(5–6): 738–62). The research for the previous article was done in January 2017. Since then, Cressingham Gardens residents have achieved very important successes that will be very useful for other campaigns. They have been successful in both the Right to Manage and the Right to Transfer. This chapter includes these new updates (latest update July 2019).
2. Henrietta Billings. 2015. 'Building of the Month', *Twentieth Century Society* (August 2015). https://c20society.org.uk/botm/cressingham-gardens-lambeth/. Accessed 15 October 2019.
3. Interview with two residents of Cressingham Gardens, 10 January 2017.

4. *R (Bokrosova) v London Borough of Lambeth* [2015] EWHC 3386 (Admin). http://www.bailii. org/ew/cases/EWHC/Admin/2015/3386.html. Accessed 23 January 2020.

5. A project team was set up by the council for 'steering and managing regeneration options and co-producing the regeneration options with the residents' (*R (Bokrosova) v London Borough of Lambeth* [2015] EWHC 3386 (Admin)). Residents were included in this project team.

6. The cabinet is an executive body of elected councillors. These are two or more elected councillors generally from the party that has won the local elections. This exists in the two executive arrangements defined by the Localism Act 2011: 'mayor and cabinet executive' and 'leader and cabinet executive'.

7. *R (Bokrosova) v London Borough of Lambeth* [2015] EWHC 3386 (Admin).

8. *R (Bokrosova) v London Borough of Lambeth* [2015] EWHC 3386 (Admin).

9. Cressingham People's Plan. 2016. http://cressinghampeoplesplan.org.uk. Accessed 21 June 2016.

10. Cressingham People's Plan. 2016.

11. *R (Plant) v Lambeth LBC* [2017] PTSR 453. http://www.bailii.org/ew/cases/EWHC/Admin/2016/3324.html. Accessed 27 January 2020.

12. *R (Plant) v Lambeth LBC* [2017] PTSR 453.

13. Interview with two residents of Cressingham Gardens, 10 January 2017.

14. Pablo Sendra. 2018. 'Assemblages for Community-Led Social Housing Regeneration: Activism, Big Society and Localism'.

15. Publication of Save Cressingham Gardens Facebook page on 22 November 2018: https://www.facebook.com/SaveCressinghamGardens. Accessed 16 July 2019.

16. These details on the Right to Manage were discussed with a Cressingham Gardens resident during the workshop we organised on 11 June 2019.

17. Ministry of Housing, Communities and Local Government. 'Right to Transfer Determinations: Cressingham Gardens Estate'. 9 July 2019. https://assets.publishing.service.gov.uk/government/uploads/system/uploads/attachment_data/file/816102/Cressingham_Gardens_determination_letter_Redacted.pdf. Accessed 16 July 2019.

18. Interview with two residents of Cressingham Gardens, 10 January 2017.

19. Interview with two residents of Cressingham Gardens, 10 January 2017.

20. Mayor of London, London Assembly. 'FOI – Estate Regeneration Schemes in London' (March 2018). https://www.london.gov.uk/about-us/governance-and-spending/sharing-our-information/freedom-information/foi-disclosure-log/foi-estate-regeneration-schemes-london. Accessed 16 July 2019.

4
Greater Carpenters Neighbourhood Forum

Carpenters Estate is a neighbourhood located near Queen Elizabeth Park in East London (fig.4.1).[1] The estate has been under consideration for demolition and redevelopment for some years, and this has generated an alliance of campaigners, residents, local businesses, London-wide networks, and organisations of students and academics working towards securing stronger participation of residents in decision-making. The neighbourhood is located in the London Borough of Newham (LBN), although the London Legacy Development Corporation (LLDC) – a Mayoral Development Corporation responsible for delivering the legacy of the London 2012 Olympic and Paralympic Games – became its planning authority in October 2012.[2] This has led to a particular situation in which the planning authority for the estate is the LLDC and the landlord is Newham Council. This has had effects on the effectiveness of the strategies followed by residents, since the LLDC was the planning authority in charge of designating the Greater Carpenters neighbourhood Forum and Neighbourhood Area. This meant that LBN, owner of the land, could not make decisions on the designation of the neighbourhood forum and neighbourhood area. This is quite a unique situation, which has made neighbourhood planning a viable strategy for contesting estate demolition.

LBN's intention to redevelop Carpenters Estate was first made public in 2004, when the council announced plans to demolish one of the towers and started relocating the residents.[3]

Tools used

The recent history of organised community opposition to redevelopment started in 2011, when LBN announced a memorandum of understanding with UCL for the construction of the UCL East campus on the site of the

Figure 4.1 Night view of the Carpenters Estate and Stratford. 2 May 2013. Image: Roel Hemkes. CC BY-SA 2.0.

Carpenters Estate.[4] A group of residents set up a campaign called Carpenters Against Regeneration Plans (CARP) to demand a 'fair deal with Newham Council'.[5]

Estate residents joined forces with local businesses to form a community planning group, supported by the London-wide alliance of campaigns and community groups Just Space, London Tenants Federation (LTF) and UCL academics and students. They developed a community plan (equivalent to a People's Plan, see chapter 12) that empowered residents and local businesses to have a say in the future of their area.[6] After UCL decided in May 2013 not to build its east campus on the Carpenters site, the community planning group continued to work together. They published a community plan in September 2013, and eventually decided to create a neighbourhood forum to turn their community plan into a Neighbourhood Plan (NP) (see chapter 9).[7] This process for making a decision to put together an NP, which comes from having previously done a non-statutory community plan, is a good example for other community groups. Residents can test the experience of putting a plan together and engage with planning before going through the NP route.

Throughout this process, the residents and local businesses in and around the Carpenters Estate have demonstrated a strong capacity to adapt to different threats and evolve from a campaign to an organisation engaging with diverse planning mechanisms. The community group that produced the original plan had emerged from the residents' campaign, CARP (Carpenters Against Regeneration Plans), which came together with a group of local businesses to form the community planning group. Believing that Newham had not carried out an appropriate consultation process for the regeneration of the housing estate, this group organised workshops and carried out a door-to-door survey that included '186 individual responses' from '157 households (more than half the remaining households on the estate) and 15 local businesses and stakeholders'.[8] The plan included proposals on housing, environmental issues, community facilities, transport, accessibility, security, local economy and community ownership.[9]

The formulation of this community plan led the neighbours to present it to the LLDC, in the process of developing its Local Plan at the time, and to continue working together in order to develop an NP to translate their proposals into statutory planning policy. This group of residents and local businesses then set up Greater Carpenters Neighbourhood Forum (GCNF), which was 'formally designated by the LLDC in July 2015'.[10] The area included not only the council housing estate, but also surrounding local businesses and new housing association developments. GCNF has achieved the listing of six Assets of Community Value (see chapter 9).[11]

In February 2017 GCNF published the fourth draft of its Neighbourhood Plan, which proposed a vision, a series of objectives, a masterplan and policies.[12] One of its objectives is 'housing refurbishment and sensitive infill', which aim to protect the existing homes and introducing new ones. This draft of the Neighbourhood Plan was published just after the Mayor of Newham 'gave the go ahead to begin the process of selecting one or more partners to bring forward the redevelopment of the estate'[13] in December 2016. These two competing initiatives from GCNF and from LBN display opposing approaches to regeneration, with the former viewing it as 'sensitive infill' and the latter describing it as 'redevelopment'. In October 2017, GCNF published the pre-submission of their Neighbourhood Plan, along with the evidence-based documents, for a consultation that took place between 30 October and 18 December 2017.[14]

At the beginning of 2018, before the municipal elections, the selection of the Labour Party candidate for the Mayor of Newham saw Robin Wales defeated by the Momentum-backed Labour candidate Rokhsana Fiaz; she was then elected Mayor of Newham in May 2018. The new Mayor brought with her a hope for a different approach to the Carpenters Estate. However, according to GCNF, attempts to engage with the Mayor of Newham did not produce a result.

On 11 June 2019, GCNF submitted their Neighbourhood Plan (NP) to the LLDC. The NP was open for consultation between 3 July and 31 August 2019 on the LLDC web page. Once the consultation period closed, the received representations were sent to the appointed examiner. At the time of writing, the examination timetable has not been published.[15] The submitted NP proposed the refurbishment of the existing homes and the preferred option for regeneration includes '650 new homes at a height of up to eight storeys, through sensitive infill. This option achieves 650 new homes, with no loss of local business or employment space and with additional community space'.[16]

As fig.4.2 shows, the strategy does not merely consist of elaborating an NP. It is, rather, using a combination of formal planning tools – neighbourhood planning, involvement in Local Plan consultation, and informal strategies – outside a formal planning framework. These informal strategies include a community plan, letter writing and various media campaigns working together seeking to secure a community-led plan.[17] One of the key strategies has been to participate in the consultation of the LLDC Local Plan. NPs cannot contradict the Local Plan, and this means that the power of neighbourhood forums is very limited if councils intend to redevelop an area. However, in this case, the planning authority in charge of the Local Plan in the Carpenters Estate area is the LLDC, not LBN.

Although the LLDC Local Plan describes the Greater Carpenters District as an 'existing mixed-use area with potential for extensive mixed-use redevelopment',[18] the neighbours, through the consultation process, managed to introduce some amendments[19] in Section 5, 'Providing housing and neighbourhoods'. The amendments refer to the entire LLDC housing strategy, not just to the Greater Carpenters District, and serve to highlight the importance of '(p)rotecting existing residential stock'.[20] In addition, the LLDC site allocation for the Greater Carpenters District states that development principles should '(c)onsider retention of existing low-rise family housing where this does not prevent the achievement of wider regeneration objectives' and '(s)upport the preparation of a Neighbourhood Plan where this conforms to the requirements of this site allocation and involves cooperation with the Council in its roles as landowner and housing authority'.[21] The combination of proposing amendments to the Local Plan and making an NP places GCNF in a stronger position as regards the possible implementation of an NP in accordance with the Local Plan, influencing future developments in the area.[22]

The campaign has developed a strong capacity to access planning expertise through its support network (see fig.4.2, which shows the different actors supporting GCNF), built up since the start of opposition to redevelopment and the drafting of the community plan. GCNF has held some of its meetings in the former Tenant Management Organisation (TMO) building and works in collaboration with Just Space and LTF. LTF has had three-year funding from Trust for London, which finished in January 2017, for 'community development support' and 'for Just Space to provide some specialist planning support around the community plan and then the Neighbourhood Plan'.[23] The same source of funding 'enabled all the participation in the LLDC Local Plan', since the funding was actually 'to support community involvement within the LLDC area',[24] not just Carpenters. Just Space and LTF are also collaborating with the UCL Department of Engineering, supporting GCNF on policy proposals on estate refurbishment and energy and water retrofit.[25]

COMMUNITY-LED REGENERATION

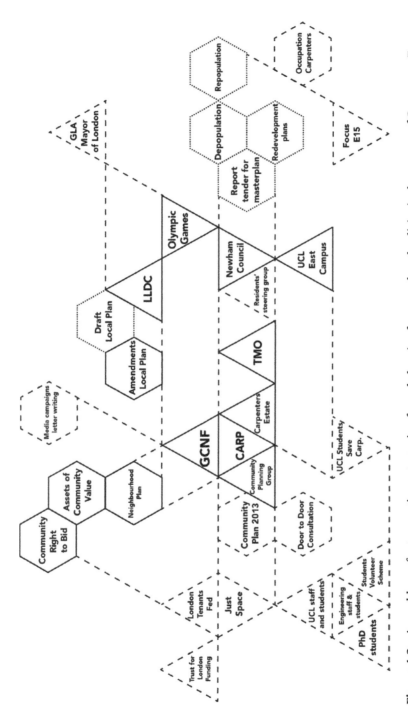

Figure 4.2 Assemblage of actors, actions, strategies, formal planning framework and policies in the context of Carpenters Estate. Triangles represent the actors involved. Those with a continuous line are directly involved; those with a dashed line show indirectly involved or supporting actors. Hexagons represent actions, strategies, formal planning tools and policies. A continuous line shows those that engage with formal planning. Those with a dashed line represent actions or strategies outside formal planning; those with a dotted line show strategies developed by public authorities.[26] Created by Pablo Sendra.

Current/future challenges

GCNF submitted its NP to the LLDC on 11 June 2019; it was then under consultation from 3 July to 31 August 2019.[27] The NP and the received representations during the consultation period have now been sent to independent examination, during which the examiner will undertake checks; they can require modifications or reject the plan. It will then be put to a local referendum (see the different steps in chapter 9).

GCNF has not managed to engage with LBN, who are the landowners of the Carpenters Estate. While the change of Mayor initially seemed promising, to date the Mayor has not yet met the forum.

Engaging with the Mayor and LBN thus seems one of the main challenges at present. The LLDC Local Plan has been reviewed and undergoes examination from 17 September 2019. The revisions, which include a new target of 2300 homes for the estate, will be contested by GCNF at the examination.

Key lessons

- Putting together a People's Plan (or community plan) can be a good strategy to test the possibility of subsequently engaging with neighbourhood planning.
- A strong support network creates opportunities for access to planning expertise.
- Combining neighbourhood planning with participating in the consultation on the Local Plan provides more possibilities for the NP to address the needs of the residents.[28]
- Community knowledge networks, including Just Space and linkages with engaged practitioners and researchers from universities, can be a key tool.

Notes

1. This chapter builds on a previous paper (Pablo Sendra. 2018. 'Assemblages for Community-Led Social Housing Regeneration: Activism, Big Society and Localism', *City* 22(5–6): 738–62.). The research for the previous article was done in January 2017. Since then, Greater Carpenters Neighbourhood Forum have submitted their Neighbourhood Plan (in June 2019). The achievement of submitting the Neighbourhood Plan can be very helpful for residents pursuing this route. This chapter is updated to July 2019.
2. London Legacy Development Corporation. 2014. 'Local Plan 2015 to 2031'. http://www. queenelizabetholympicpark.co.uk/~/media/lldc/local%20plan/local%20plan%20aug14/ local%20plan.pdf. Accessed 17 July 2019.

3. Alexandre Frediani, Stephanie Butcher and Paul Watt, eds. 2013. *Regeneration and Well-Being in East London: Stories from Carpenters Estate*. London: The Bartlett Development Planning Unit, UCL. https://issuu.com/dpu-ucl/docs/carpenters-estate-london. Accessed 23 January 2020.

4. Frediani, Butcher and Watt, eds, 2013. *Regeneration and Well-Being in East London: Stories from Carpenters Estate*.

5. Save Carpenters. https://savecarpenters.wordpress.com/about/. Accessed 28 February 2017.

6. Just Space. 2015. *London For All! A Handbook for Community and Small Business Groups Fighting to Retain Workspace for London's Diverse Economies*. London: Just Space and New Economics Foundation.

7. Just Space. 2015. *London For All! A Handbook for Community and Small Business Groups Fighting to Retain Workspace for London's Diverse Economies*.

8. Greater Carpenters Neighbourhood Forum. 2013. 'Carpenters Community Plan 2013: Preparation and Consultation Report'. https://greatercarpenterscouk.files.wordpress.com/2015/06/carpenters-community-plan-preparation-and-consultation-report.pdf. Accessed 17 July 2019.

9. Greater Carpenters Neighbourhood Forum. 2013. 'Carpenters Community Plan 2013: Preparation and Consultation Report'.

10. Greater Carpenters Neighbourhood Forum. 'Achievements'. https://greater-carpenters.co.uk/our-work/achievements/. Accessed 4 December 2017.

11. Greater Carpenters Neighbourhood Forum. 'Assets of Community Value'. https://greater-carpenters.co.uk/our-work/achievements/assets-of-community-value/. Accessed 17 July 2017.

12. Greater Carpenters Neighbourhood Forum. 2017. 'Greater Carpenters Neighbourhood Plan. 4th Draft, 6th February 2017'. https://greater-carpenters.co.uk/our-work/greater-carpenters-neighbourhood-plan/. Accessed 23 January 2020.

13. London Borough of Newham. 2017. 'Carpenters Estate Newsletter Update – March 2017'. https://www.newham.gov.uk/Documents/Business/CarpentersEstateNewsletterUpdate-March2017.pdf. Accessed 23 January 2020.

14. Greater Carpenters Neighbourhood Forum. 2017. 'Pre-submission Neighbourhood Plan & Evidence Based Documents'. https://greater-carpenters.co.uk/2017/10/29/consultation-draft-stage-2017/. Accessed 17 July 2019.

15. London Legacy Development Corporation. 2019. 'Neighbourhood Planning'. https://www.queenelizabetholympicpark.co.uk/planning-authority/planning-policy/neighbourhood-planning, Accessed 17 July 2019.

16. Greater Carpenters Neighbourhood Forum. 2019. 'Greater Carpenters Neighbourhood Plan 2019–2028. Submission Version May 2019', p. 20. https://greater-carpenters.co.uk/our-work/greater-carpenters-neighbourhood-plan/. Accessed 23 January 2020.

17. Cecil Sagoe. 2016. 'One Tool Amongst Many: Considering the Political Potential of Neighbourhood Planning for the Greater Carpenters Neighbourhood, London', *Architecture, Media, Politics and Society* 9(3): 1–20.

18. London Legacy Development Corporation. 2014. 'Local Plan 2015 to 2031', 200.

19. Sagoe. 2016. 'One Tool Amongst Many: Considering the Political Potential of Neighbourhood Planning for the Greater Carpenters Neighbourhood, London', 12.

20. London Legacy Development Corporation. 2014. 'Local Plan 2015 to 2031', 44.

21. London Legacy Development Corporation. 2015. 'Site Allocation SA3.4 – Greater Carpenters District'. http://www.queenelizabetholympicpark.co.uk/-/media/lldc/local-plan/31-march/site-allocation-sa34-response-to-inspector-31st-march-2015.ashx?la=en. Accessed 23 January 2020.

22. Sagoe. 2016. 'One Tool Amongst Many: Considering the Political Potential of Neighbourhood Planning for the Greater Carpenters Neighbourhood, London'.

23. Interview with Richard Lee, Just Space coordinator, 18 January 2017.

24. Interview with Richard Lee, Just Space coordinator, 18 January 2017.

25. Interview with Richard Lee, Just Space coordinator, 18 January 2017. See also 'Greater Carpenters Neighbourhood Forum. 2017'. Greater Carpenters Neighbourhood Plan. 4th Draft, February 2017.

26. Sendra. 2018. 'Assemblages for Community-Led Social Housing Regeneration: Activism, Big Society and Localism'.

27. London Legacy Development Corporation. 2019. 'Neighbourhood Planning'. https://www.queenelizabetholympicpark.co.uk/planning-authority/planning-policy/neighbourhood-planning. Accessed 23 January 2020.

28. Sagoe. 2016. 'One Tool Amongst Many: Considering the Political Potential of Neighbourhood Planning for the Greater Carpenters Neighbourhood, London'.

5
Focus E15

This campaign differs from the others presented in this book.[1] Rather than presenting a group of residents fighting against the demolition of their housing estate, it presents a group of women who, fighting against their eviction from temporary accommodation in the London Borough of Newham (LBN), have since become one of the strongest, most vocal housing campaigns in the UK. The reason for their inclusion in this book is to provide an example of the effect that direct action and informal strategies can have on housing campaigns. They also provide a good example of how a housing campaign can evolve, create and establish alliances with other campaigns, and provide support to people experiencing similar housing struggles.

The group's history and trajectory also provide an example that demonstrates the reality of what is needed to encourage and nurture the confidence to take initial political steps and to be able to act, moving as a group from an oppositional to a propositional mode of campaigning. The initial meeting of the mothers of Focus E15 with more experienced campaigners led to a very strong unit able to take that first action. The experienced campaigners had been involved in the Counihan-Sanchez Housing Campaign[2] as well as earlier political struggles such as the anti-apartheid movement in the 1980s.[3] What is very significant is the political belief held throughout the campaign that those directly affected should be given the tools to ensure they increase their ability and confidence to sustain their own campaign. Another interesting point is how the group has connected with a wider history of campaigning. For example, one of the activists reported that as the campaign grew and they read more history, they saw that what they were doing was exactly what Sylvia Pankhurst and the East London Federation of Suffragettes had done a century earlier in East London.[4]

Like Greater Carpenters Neighbourhood Forum (GCNF) and People's Empowerment Alliance for Custom House (PEACH), this campaign is located in the London Borough of Newham (LBN). A very important moment in their contestation related to the Carpenters Estate – where GCNF is located – although the campaign goes beyond fighting for a particular place and has become a broader campaign against social cleansing.[5] The origins of Focus E15 are quite different from that of the GCNF and other groups discussed in this book. Focus E15 is a group of young mothers who were living in a hostel for young people experiencing homelessness. This hostel suffered a £40,000 cut in funding in 2013 and, as a result, the 'mother and baby unit' of the hostel in Newham was closed. The tenants of this unit were served an eviction notice, and when one of them sought help from the council to find accommodation within the borough, she was told that she should find private accommodation outside London,[6] as it was not possible to rehouse her in Newham.

Following this negative response, one of the young women complained to her own mother (a school worker in Newham). She advised her daughter that 'you need to speak to the other mums and get together to challenge this'. So, through communicating with each other, a group of 29 mothers, all of whom had received eviction notices, started to organise themselves. The women mounted a petition for them and their children to be rehoused in Newham. They also met another group of women from the Revolutionary Communist Group, who were running a stall against the bedroom tax, and asked them for advice on campaigning. This chance encounter[7] helped the group of mothers to develop the political confidence and backing to take determined action, led by them and supported by others.

Tools used

The group started a series of direct actions, such as occupying council offices and attending events organised by the council. Through these actions they gained public support and the council agreed to rehouse them within the local area.[8] The women decided to keep fighting using the slogan 'Social housing, not social cleansing'[9] and continued to hold their weekly stall in Stratford. On the first anniversary of their campaign, in September 2014, they carried out the 'political occupation' (fig.5.1) of an empty housing block on the Carpenters Estate. This action was to focus attention on 'the fact that people are being forced out of London due to a lack of affordable housing while huge numbers of perfectly good social housing units sit empty'.[10]

The occupation had a major impact in the media and finally led to the council deciding to repopulate 40 empty homes on the estate. It also drew attention to how Newham Council had treated the Focus E15

Figure 5.1 Focus E15's political occupation of an empty housing block on the Carpenters Estate. 27 September 2014. Image: danstowell (flickr). CC BY-SA 2.0.

mothers, leading to a public apology from the Mayor of Newham which was published in *The Guardian* on 6 October 2014.[11] At the time of writing, the campaign continues to hold its weekly stalls every Saturday. It also has a space, Sylvia's Corner, where events are organised and support is provided to people experiencing housing difficulties.

Focus E15 differs from other groups discussed in this book in that the campaign has not taken the form of a formal organisation. It has remained deliberately 'fluid',[12] consisting of a group made up of different people engaging at different times. The campaign started with 29 young mothers, who created an informal alliance with a local group associated with the Revolutionary Communist Group (RCG);[13] together they organised a joint weekly stall. Since then, volunteers have joined the campaign, and academics and professionals have provided support. As of 2017, only two of the mothers from those initially involved are still part of the core campaign.[14] However, since the initial victory of late 2013 that kept 29 mothers housed in Newham, a succession of families and individuals directly affected by homelessness and facing social cleansing from the borough have become involved in the campaign. According to one of the volunteers, rather than setting up any kind of formal organisation, the campaign wants to remain focused on housing. It prefers to involve a flexible, dynamic group of people, in order to preserve the fluidity and radical nature of the original group and to adapt to an uncertain future.[15]

As shown in fig.5.2, three combinations of actions and alliances have made this campaign really strong and able to resist and contest a range of housing injustices. These are the 'political occupation' of the block at the Carpenters Estate, the weekly stall and Sylvia's Corner.

The 'political occupation' of a housing block on the Carpenters Estate had the strongest impact in the media, as well as a tangible impact on the defence of social housing. It highlighted the fact that fit-for-purpose homes were being left empty by the council despite the great demand for social housing. This action was successful in pressuring the council to re-occupy 40 empty homes. It proved a veritable boost to the campaign, since it demonstrated clearly that 'grassroots action can work'.[16]

The weekly stall started with an alliance with the RCG, previously in charge of an anti-austerity stall,[17] and it has been very important for holding their petitions, fundraising and to ensure a constant presence on the streets, keeping the campaign alive.

Sylvia's Corner, named after Sylvia Pankhurst, the suffragette and East End-based organiser, is a space in a corner shop on a residential street in Stratford.[18] It is used to store campaigning materials, hold monthly meetings open to the public and organise drop-in sessions to help people confronting housing issues.[19] Through fundraising and donations, the group has managed to rent this space, giving them a focal meeting point where the problems of housing and gentrification can be tackled. Sylvia's Corner also hosts other groups' events, which helps to connect with other campaigns and housing movements.

Therefore, some traits of Focus E15's structure have made it adaptable and dynamic. This flexibility may arise in part from Focus E15's explicit feminism and deeply rooted resistance to hierarchy. This factor has permeated into its alliance with different groups, campaigns and network, and along with the three strategies explained above – that is to say, action with strong media impact, constant presence on the streets and a meeting point in a corner shop – have made Focus E15 a point of reference among housing campaigns. It provides a unique range of different kinds of capabilities in campaigning for social housing. In July 2019, six years after it started, the group has a strong presence in many housing demonstrations. It also provides support to different causes and takes part in numerous events on housing activism.

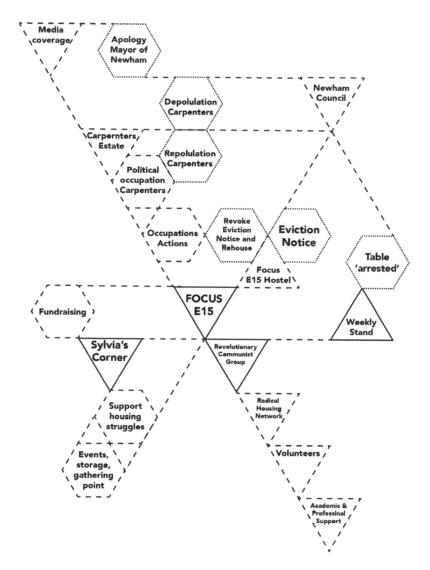

Figure 5.2 Assemblage of actors, actions and strategies in Focus E15 campaign. Triangles represent the actors involved. Those with a continuous line are directly involved; those with a dashed line are indirectly involved or supporting actors. Hexagons represent actions, strategies, formal planning tools and policies. A continuous line shows those that engage with formal planning. Those with a dashed line represent actions or strategies outside formal planning, while a dotted line shows strategies developed by public authorities.[20] Created by Pablo Sendra.

Current and future challenges

Focus E15 has consolidated its role in the community, with a regular stall, small office space and its focus on housing rights and struggles against the impact of austerity measures, especially in housing. Accounts of its ongoing work can be found on the group's blog, FocusE15.org. This is both an important resource and focus of its work, as the blog is a tool in itself, for its campaign. It has been running for over five years and details the stories of homeless families and individuals, with a focus on London and housing activism in support of these families.

The blog has also served as a chronicle of Focus E15's own campaigns and alliances. For example, for the last six months, Focus E15 has been organising with families from Brimstone House (the renamed focus E15 hostel, where the campaign started) to launch a large-scale legal complaint against Newham Council with regard to temporary accommodation. The legal complaint was presented by a deputation of activists and residents to the Mayor at a full meeting of Newham Council,[21] and the group is now embarking on a historic legal challenge.[22]

Key lessons

- Actions that attract media attention can have immediate effect and force local authorities to react.
- A weekly presence on the streets makes the campaign stronger.
- A dedicated space for the campaign contributes helps to run activities and generate networks of support with other campaigns and people affected by housing issues.
- Keeping the campaign as an informal organisation gives a lot of flexibility for tackling a diverse range of actions.

For the fifth anniversary of Focus E15 the group reflected on, discussed and debated the lessons they had learned themselves from campaigning. As a result, they produced a wide-ranging list of lessons that were, in their words, a sincere and accurate reflection of their key lessons for other campaigners. These were as follows:[23]

- Take direct action: it is empowering, provocative but also informative since it highlights and communicates important issues to the wider community. Direct action can take many forms, such as protesting at council meetings, holding a space on the streets, taking a march from the pavement to the road and chanting outside the housing or council offices.

- Together we are stronger and solidarity is vital – but also ensure that people's individual voices are heard, since more people and more support will make the campaigning easier. The focus, however, should be to include those most affected and to give them a voice.
- Speaking truth to power is key for any alliance that Focus E15 makes. The group is clearly left-leaning, but not allied to any current electoral party and is independent, since it has observed that many of the struggles for housing occur in Labour-run councils. The crucial thing for the campaign is thus to connect with any individuals, groups or organisations who are challenging those in power over better housing conditions.
- One struggle! One fight! It is essential to link with struggles dealing with housing across the world, from Palestine to Venezuela, and to learn from one another about the political dimensions of the struggle as well as practical tactics used.
- Art is a political tool. It can be used by campaigners in creative ways, from banners and chants, songs and slogans, to plays and films on housing campaigns. These are all forms of creative communication and an important way to reach more people.
- Be a housing expert – or know one! It is crucial to be able to understand the system, not only to discover what the policies do and the legalities of the system, but also to learn more broadly why the housing system is the way it is, how markets function and what the role of the state is. Find out where to find advice, assistance and support, especially with legal matters, early on. Linking up with networks of housing groups as well as finding and distributing reading material produced by groups such as Architects for Social Housing[24] is important.
- Keep your spirits up, both as campaigners and also as individuals faced with the political and housing struggles. Campaigning has to be fun so making it a social event, with music, theatre, dance, colour, food sharing and other activities such as face-painting helps.
- Networking and building with other groups has been important over the last five years – not only to grow the support for Focus E15, but also to learn from other groups. Have an open, democratic structure for meetings, but also create spaces of encounter, such as the stall where links with other local groups can be made.
- Learning from history has introduced a different dimension of time to the campaign, from the stories of Sylvia Pankhurst and the building of the suffrage movement to Mrs Barbour of the Glasgow Rent Strikes in 1915.

- There is room for everyone – but no room for racism! Inclusiveness in campaigning has been important, but racism cannot be tolerated. In housing campaigns, one can sometimes hear on the streets that the problems have been caused by immigration. This is something that Focus E15 has been constantly speaking out against, and it should also be applied to wider social struggles.

Notes

1. This chapter builds on a previous paper (Pablo Sendra. 2018. 'Assemblages for Community-Led Social Housing Regeneration: Activism, Big Society and Localism', *City* 22(5–6): 738–62). The research for the previous article was done in January 2017. The content of the paper has been adapted and updated for the purpose of this book and includes contributions and edits on our previous research by Sakia O'Hara, campaigner with Focus E15.
2. The Counihan-Sanchez Campaign in Brent was a housing campaign that emerged from the experience of the Counihan-Sanchez family. Their household income was not sufficient to cover the cost of renting in the private sector and they relied on housing benefits to make ends meet. Their housing benefit was suddenly cut completely, which caused the family to fall into arrears and led to their eviction. The campaign, which brought together an alliance of housing and anti-austerity activists, demanded that Brent Council should stop the implementation of cuts to local services and use their budget to build more social housing. Eventually, the pressure by the campaign won back the family's housing benefits, but (at the time of the documentary below) they were still living in temporary, overcrowded accommodation in Ealing, far away from the children's schools. See the short documentary 'TheHousingForAll'. *Housing 4 The Counihan's Housing 4 All!* (documentary film, 2013). https://www.youtube.com/watch?time_continue=6&v=JgsGaCI1t-o. Accessed 30 July 2019.
3. See Gavin Brown. 2014. 'Objecting to Apartheid: Building a Non-stop Protest in 1980s' London', *V&A Blog* (16 May 2014). https://www.vam.ac.uk/blog/disobedient-objects/objecting-apartheid-building-non-stop-protest-1980s-london. Accessed 30 July 2019.
4. In correspondence with Sakia O'Hara, campaigner with Focus E15 on 29 July 2019.
5. Paul Watt. 2016. 'A Nomadic War Machine in the Metropolis: En/countering London's 21st-century Housing Crisis with Focus E15', *City* 20 (2): 297–320.
6. Interview with Ella Bradbury, volunteer from Focus E15 campaign, 8 January 2017.
7. Paul Watt. 2016. 'A Nomadic War Machine in the Metropolis: En/countering London's 21st-century Housing Crisis with Focus E15', *City* 20 (2): 297–320.
8. Interview with Ella Bradbury, 8 January 2017.
9. Focus E15 Campaign. 'About Us'. https://focuse15.org/about. Accessed 6 June 2017.
10. Focus E15 Campaign. 'E15 Open House Occupation'. https://focuse15.org/e15-open-house-occupation. Accessed 6 June 2017.
11. Robin Wales. 2014. 'I Apologise to the Focus E15 Families, but this is a London Housing Crisis', *The Guardian* (6 October 2014). https://www.theguardian.com/commentisfree/2014/oct/06/apologise-focus-e15-london-housing-crisis-newham. Accessed 6 June 2017.
12. Interview with Ella Bradbury, 8 January 2017.
13. See how Watt explains this alliance between Focus E15 and RCG as an 'assemblage'. Watt. 2016. 'A Nomadic War Machine in the Metropolis: En/countering London's 21st-century Housing Crisis with Focus E15'.
14. Interview with Ella Bradbury, 8 January 2017.
15. Interview with Ella Bradbury, 8 January 2017.
16. Sendra. 2018. 'Assemblages for Community-Led Social Housing Regeneration: Activism, Big Society and Localism'.
17. Interview with Ella Bradbury, 8 January 2017.
18. Watt. 2016. 'A Nomadic War Machine in the Metropolis: En/countering London's 21st-century Housing Crisis with Focus E15', 304.

19. Focus E15 Campaign. 'Sylvia's Corner'. https://focuse15.org/sylvias-corner/. Accessed 6 June 2017.
20. Interview with Ella Bradbury, 8 January 2017.
21. Focus E15 Campaign. 2019. 'Newham Residents' Complaint to Mayor at Full Council Meeting,' 16 July 2019. https://focuse15.org/2019/07/16/newham-residents-complaint-to-mayor-at-full-council-meeting, Accessed 30 July 2019.
22. Focus E15 Campaign. 2019. 'Legal Complaint Served – This Could Go to the High Court say Public Interest Law Centre'. 23 July 2019. https://focuse15.org/2019/07/23/legal-complaint-served-this-could-go-to-the-high-court-says-public-interest-law-centre. Accessed 30 July 2019.
23. The following 10 points have been taken from Focus E15 as suggested by Sakia O'Hara, campaigner from Focus E15, in part because they reflect very well what the group has experienced and thought about and in part because of their relevance to other housing campaigns and wider political struggles. Focus E15 Campaign, '10 Things to Learn from Focus E15 Campaign'. https://focuse15.org/2018/09/30/10-things-to-learn-from-focus-e15-campaign. Accessed 30 July 2019.
24. Architects for Social Housing. https://architectsforsocialhousing.co.uk. Accessed 30 July 2019.

6
People's Empowerment Alliance for Custom House

People's Empowerment Alliance for Custom House (PEACH) is a group of residents and local businesses located in Custom House, an area in the London Borough of Newham (LBN) – the same local authority as Greater Carpenters Neighbourhood Forum and Focus E15. The difference between PEACH and other case studies discussed in this book is that PEACH is not fighting against demolition and redevelopment, but making sure that all residents 'have a home at the end of it'.[1] PEACH started in 2013 when a group of residents, local leaders, church leaders and a local councillor came together and created the group. The community was successful in securing £1m in grant funding from Big Local (a part of the National Lottery Fund which targets deprived communities), to be spent over 10 years. Since Custom House was a deprived area that had not received investment for many years and already had a steering group of residents, it became one of the 150 areas across the UK to receive such funding to invest in local projects.

The first step was to decide what the funds could be used for. While initial discussions focused on small businesses and local projects, as other Big Local areas had done, it was quickly realised that the funds would be rapidly disbursed and would have little impact on the local area.[2] The group thus made 'a conscious decision to use community organising as (…) the method of change'.[3] Uniquely for a community group that has received a big pot of funding, the grant was initially used for hiring community organisers for the purpose of 'building the power of the community'.[4] The first community organiser helped with both the door-knocking campaign and meeting residents. The community subsequently voted for the four key topics that PEACH would concentrate on: jobs, housing, safety and health.

The council's plans for regeneration were initiated well before PEACH was founded. While residents started to hear about these proposals in the early 2000s, information since then has not been consistent. The regeneration of Custom House is part of a larger programme led by LBN called 'Custom House and Canning Town Regeneration' which involves 19 different areas. Some of this regeneration had already occurred in Canning Town, but the reduced proportion of social housing in the regeneration areas alerted residents and raised their concerns about housing, one of PEACH's key topics.

Tools used

One of the key strategies for PEACH is community organising[5] (discussed in Part III, 'Next Challenges for Community-Led Regeneration'). As noted above, PEACH made an important initial decision to spend their funding mainly on community organising, with the specific aim of strengthening the resident and local business voice. One of the community organisers and one of the founder members of PEACH were interviewed in November 2017, at the time when they had six community organisers (one working full time, and the others working part time). These community organisers were responsible for the different projects that PEACH were running. They are not members of the steering committee, but they coordinate projects, organise events and help with the door-knocking and other activities to bring the community together. The interviewee defines PEACH's relationship with the council as 'respectful'.[6] They think it is important to keep a respectful relationship with those who have decision-making power in order to achieve change. At the same time, they need to apply pressure on occasion to ensure that the voices of the community are heard.

Community organising and the work of dedicated residents and shopkeepers have made possible a very well-developed structure of governance. PEACH's steering committee, formed of residents and shopkeepers, is the body that makes decisions and decides on the allocation of financial resources. In addition to the steering committee, there are different 'projects', such as the Housing Club, the Workers Coop or the Parents' Group, among others. Two people from each project sit on the steering group and all projects are represented in this way.

The Housing Club 'project' deals with the regeneration of Custom House; as of November 2017, it had 114 members who pay £1 each to join. The group meets regularly, discusses what is happening and takes appropriate action. Through that group, PEACH decided in December

2015 to prepare their own community-led plan (equivalent to a People's Plan, chapter 12) in order to develop a vision of what the community wanted for the area. Although the council already had a masterplan dating from 2007, as well as a Supplementary Planning Document (SPD) for the whole area of Custom House and Canning Town from 2008, the community wanted to prepare an alternative plan in which they could present their own vision.

During 2016 a team of 10 people, consisting of six community organisers and four architects, was hired to work on the community-led plan. Each of the team members was hired for one day a week and received the same hourly rate, while five of the six community organisers were local people. The team was thus very transversal. There was little differentiation between the work of the architects and that of the community organisers, with the architects contributing to the door-knocking campaign and other types of work normally the responsibility of community organisers.

The process for preparing the plan began with door-knocking and workshops which were hosted in different community buildings. From this initial work, three main themes emerged: housing, economy of services, and community and public space. Separate workshops were then held for each of the topics in order to identify solutions, not just problems, and a series of aims and principles were identified for each of the themes.

Further work on the community-led plan continued from April to September 2017, particularly through the Housing Club. It held meetings to discuss issues of possible concern, such as the massing and height of the buildings. People did not want tower blocks, so the community plans proposed buildings of mainly four to six storeys. These were mostly perimeter blocks with shared courtyards and gardens in the middle, the latter features being a priority for the community members. The masterplan proposed many changes to the public spaces and communal areas, including shops with housing above, a community centre with housing above, and a market square. The team produced two versions of the community-led plan, one that proposed substantial refurbishment and another one that included full demolition. The demolition option would start with building housing in one of the sites for the people to be moved first. This strategy would allow a phased demolition, in which people have to move only once.

In July 2017 PEACH asked the council to organise a monthly collaboration workshop, with a lead consultant from the council and PEACH as a partner in the process. This was agreed. In September 2017 the team presented the draft community-led plan to a meeting of the Housing Club; over 50 members attended and voted to support the plan and present it to the council. In November 2017 PEACH showed the community-led plan to the council. The result of the meeting was very positive. At that time the council told PEACH they were going to look for a design team and that they would include PEACH's community-led plans as part of the brief. PEACH contributed to the evaluation criteria for choosing the design team, one of the criteria being that the successful bidder should have experience of previous work with communities.

Current and future challenges

In May 2018 the mayorship of Newham changed; it remained Labour, but the new Mayor was from a different faction of the party. PEACH has developed a good relationship with the new Mayor. The council has committed to a co-production process with PEACH and to a ballot. This co-production consists of two parts. First, the conditions for the project have been prepared together with community representatives. Half of the regeneration steering group are community representatives. There are still some questions about whether that steering committee is an advisory group or a decision-making body, but the relationship between LBN and PEACH can be seen as close to a 'partnership' in the terms described in Arnstein's 'ladder of participation'.[7]

PEACH has also created a Community Land Trust (CLT): E16 CLT. Although no agreement has been reached on the role that E16 CLT will have in the delivery of affordable housing, the CLT is working towards a goal of delivering affordable housing in the regeneration area. This is significant as the Mayor of Newham has a manifesto commitment to support the establishment of a Community Land Trust in the borough. There is an agreement, about E16 CLT starting to manage up to 10 empty properties, which could be a pilot project as they set up as a CLT.[8]

Through campaigning and adopting a negotiating attitude towards the council, PEACH has managed to influence the decision-making process. It has been able to co-produce the brief for the regeneration project with the council, together with residents and the architects responsible for the design. The latter were chosen by a panel composed of two council officers and two elected community representatives. PEACH has also managed to have six people from its community, 50 per cent representation, on the steering group; these representatives are elected by residents in a local vote.[9] One of the main challenges that PEACH will face is to sustain that partnership, and to ensure that the voices of the community continue to be heard and considered in further regeneration. There are also questions on the decision-making power of the steering group, which they will have to keep negotiating with the council.

Key lessons

- Having a 'respectful' relationship with the council and, at the same time, being ready to put pressure on them for the community to have decision-making powers is a good strategy, enabling a group to work towards a partnership with the local authority.
- Investing funds and resources in community organising is very important to ensure the community has a stronger voice.
- A People's Plan is an effective way to bring together a collective vision from the community. It is less burdensome, in terms of time and resources needed, than a Neighbourhood Plan and, although non-statutory, can be used to influence decision-making.
- Creating your own team of community organisers and architects to put together a community-led plan gives further community control for making decisions.

Notes

1. Interview with community organiser Dan Barron and with one of the founder members of PEACH, 16 November 2017. This quote is from the founder member of PEACH.
2. Interview with community organiser Dan Barron and with one of the founder members of PEACH, 16 November 2017. This quote is from the founder member of PEACH.
3. Interview with community organiser Dan Barron, 16 November 2017.
4. Interview with community organiser Dan Barron, 16 November 2017.
5. All of this information comes from an interview with Dan Barron, the community organiser responsible for the Housing Club, 16 November 2017. Updates after November 2017 come from a talk Dan Barron gave in our final event on 11 June 2019.
6. Interview with Dan Barron, the community organiser responsible for the Housing Club, 16 November 2017.
7. Sherry Phyllis Arnstein. 1969. 'A Ladder of Citizen Participation', *Journal of the American Planning Association* 35(4): 216–224.
8. This paragraph comes from the talk that Dan Barron, community organiser at PEACH, gave in our final workshop on 11 June 2019, and from correspondence with him, 31 July 2019.
9. From correspondence with Dan Barron from PEACH, 1 August 2019.

7
Alexandra and Ainsworth Estates

Alexandra and Ainsworth Estates are located in the London Borough of Camden (LBC).[1] The estates include the iconic brutalist Grade II* listed buildings on Alexandra Road (fig.7.1), designed by RIBA Royal Gold Medal-winning architect Neave Brown in 1968 and built in 1978. They are low-rise, high-density social housing, a typology that emerged in the late 1960s and 1970s as a reaction to tower blocks.[2]

This case study is very different from the others discussed in the book. Alexandra Road is not under threat of demolition, although it does face other challenges, principally because it is a Grade II* listed set of buildings. The Grade II* category, defined by Historic England as 'particularly important buildings of more than special interest',[3] means that '... there will be extra control over what changes can be made to a building's interior and exterior. Owners will need to apply for Listed Building Consent for most types of work that affect the "special architectural or historic interest" of their home'.[4] This makes undertaking any change on the building very difficult.

The campaign to list the building was led by Elizabeth Knowles, an estate resident, and Christopher Dean of DOCOMOMO.[5] They succeeded in obtaining the Grade II* listing in August 1993,[6] thus protecting the buildings from any change. More recently the residents, working in partnership with LBC, succeeded in getting Heritage Lottery Fund financing to refurbish Alexandra Road Park (fig.7.2), a public green space within the estate, and the funds covered both the design and construction.

One of the main challenges they are currently facing is the refurbishment of the heating arrangements – currently a unique, centralised system distributed through a network of pipes embedded in the walls between each house. Consequently the heating is inevitably shared between the homes. The council views such a centralised system as inefficient, and it plans to change the system from collective to individual. This

Figure 7.1 Alexandra Road. September 2015. Image: Pablo Sendra.

would require moving from the current system integrated in the walls to another one, such as a radiator-based system. In addition to affecting the interior design of the flats, this would also imply that everyone is responsible for their own heating bills, which risks becoming a burden for low-income tenants. Therefore residents are contesting this proposal because of the effect that it could have on some tenants. They also believe that the current inefficiency is not due to the heating system itself, but rather to the poor insulation of the flats. This has led to some discussions between residents and the council concerning the change of heating system and the quality of the ongoing maintenance work, as well as the process of procuring the works, both those that are in progress as well as any future work.[7]

Tools used

Two unique tools feature in this case study. The first one is the listing of the estate, which has successfully protected it from demolition. The second one is applying for – and managing to get – Heritage Lottery Fund financing for the restoration of Alexandra Road Park.

Listing buildings within a housing estate is a strategy that can protect the estate against demolition. However, it does not necessarily protect residents against displacement, as the case of Balfron Tower in Tower Hamlets demonstrates. In the case of Balfron Tower, also a listed building, social housing tenants were moved out of their flats before the housing association, in a joint venture with private developers, started the refurbishment and turned all the flats into private homes.[8]

In the case of Alexandra Road, the campaign for listing the buildings succeeded in getting the buildings listed as Grade II* in 1993. Alexandra Road became the first modernist social housing estate to be listed by Historic England;[9] others have followed. The estate is currently well-preserved and represents an important set of buildings in the history of modern architecture in Britain. Every year the estate participates in the Open House event organised by Open City. It has also been featured in many films and television series because of its iconic and unusual street and building layout.

Listing the building also allowed an opportunity to apply for a sum from the Heritage Lottery Fund to restore Alexandra Road Park. This park within the estate was designed by Neave Brown, with Janet Jack as

Figure 7.2 Alexandra Road Park after restoration. September 2015. Image: Pablo Sendra.

landscape architect, between 1972 and 1978. It is part of the Alexandra Road Conservation Area.[10] In 2010 a group of residents came together with the aim of restoring the park. They applied to the Heritage Lottery Fund's 'Parks for People' programme,[11] which awards '(g)rants for projects that regenerate historic public parks and cemeteries'.[12] The application to this programme had two stages. First, they applied for funding for the development of the project. Second, once they had a project in partnership with LBC and including a team of professionals, they applied for, and successfully obtained, funding for restoring the park. The restoration finished in July 2015. It included 'new purpose made playgrounds', 'restoring all the paths' and 'revitalising the planting'.[13] The park reopened in September 2015. This is a good example of an initiative of maintenance and refurbishment works started by residents, who then got the council on board to work in partnership with them on the project; the council in turn appointed a project manager and dealt with the finance and management of the project.[14]

The more recent concerns of residents regarding their estate are related to issues of repairs and maintenance, and there are various ongoing disputes with the council. The main issue is over the repair or change of the heating system and the works carried out by the 'Better Homes' programme. As already indicated, the council intends to change the heating system from collective to individual arrangements. This requires altering the current heating pipe system, embedded in the concrete walls between homes, to an individual, home-based radiator system. As noted, residents argue that the current inefficiency lies not as much in the heating system, but rather in the buildings' poor insulation. They also fear that changing the heating system would impact the energy bills of low-income tenants (with potential implications for fuel poverty); it could also affect the heritage significance of the building. Residents are thus claiming that the council should change its procurement process and assess the improvement of the insulation of the buildings before considering changing the heating system itself.[15]

Some of the residents also noticed that the work being carried out by LBC in some flats as part of the 'Better Homes' programme was destroying some of the protected interior design of the buildings. They denounced it on Twitter, talked to architectural digital magazines[16] and discussed the situation with DOCOMOMO. After an inspection from DOCOMOMO, the council decided to reappoint the architectural practice that had prepared the works in order to supervise the ongoing works. This result demonstrates the importance of residents safeguarding their own heritage and speaking out when things are not done right. Here they used social media and architectural media to make their voices heard and collaborated with the architectural heritage organisation DOCOMOMO.[17]

Current/next challenges

The main ongoing challenges facing the Alexandra and Ainsworth Estates are the maintenance of the buildings and the possible implications of changing the heating system. Regarding the maintenance of the buildings, the residents have managed to get the council to appoint the architects who designed the repair works to undertake the supervision of the works. As for the heating system, residents are trying to push the council to prioritise the insulation of the buildings, believing that this would significantly increase their energy efficiency.[18]

Key lessons

- Applying[19] successfully to list a building can protect it from demolition and major changes.
- Living in a listed estate brings opportunities for funding from the Heritage Lottery Fund.
- Demonstrating the capacity of self-organisation and applying for funding can bring the local authority on board, support the building of partnerships and facilitate a project initiated by the community.
- Scrutiny is needed by residents of the repairs and maintenance works carried out by the local authority, from the procurement process to the design project and through to the actual works.
- Denouncing bad practices relating to architectural heritage to architectural media and organisations in support of built heritage can have its positive effects.

Notes

1. The blog of the Alexandra and Ainsworth Estates Tenants and Residents Association is a useful resource of the history and current activities on the estate: Alexandra and Ainsworth Estates Tenants and Residents Association. http://alexandraandainsworth.org. Accessed 31 July 2019.
2. Alexandra and Ainsworth Estates Tenants and Residents Association: Lefkos Kyriacou (resident and architect). n.d. 'A Short History of the Alexandra and Ainsworth Estate'. http://alexandraandainsworth.org/estate-history-3. Accessed 26 July 2019.

3. Historic England. 2019. 'Listed Building'. https://historicengland.org.uk/listing/what-is-designation/listed-buildings/. Accessed 26 July 2019.
4. Historic England. 2019. 'Living in a Grade I, Grade II* or Grade II Listed Building'. https://historicengland.org.uk/advice/your-home/owning-historic-property/listed-building/. Accessed 26 July 2019.
5. DOCOMOMO is an international, non-profit, networked organisation for the protection of modernist architecture. Its full title is International Committee for Documentation and Conservation of Buildings, Sites and Neighbourhoods of the Modern Movement, and it has a UK chapter.
6. Email exchange with Elizabeth Knowles, resident who co-led the listing of the estate, 28 July 2019.
7. Conversation with Elena Besussi, resident in Alexandra and Ainsworth Estates, June 2019.
8. Anna Minton. 2018. 'The Price of Regeneration', *Places Journal*. https://placesjournal.org/article/the-price-of-regeneration-in-london. Accessed 18 November 2019.
9. Alexandra and Ainsworth Estates Tenants and Residents Association: Lefkos Kyriacou (resident and architect). n.d. 'A Short History of the Alexandra and Ainsworth Estate'.
10. Friends of Alexandra Road Park. https://friendsofalexandraroadpark.com. Accessed 26 July 2019.
11. Friends of Alexandra Park. 2019. 'Restoring the Park'. https://friendsofalexandraroadpark.com/about/restoring-the-park/. Accessed 26 July 2019.
12. The National Lottery Community Fund. n.d. 'Parks for People'. https://www.tnlcommunity-fund.org.uk/funding/programmes/parks-for-people#section-2. Accessed 27 July 2019.
13. Friends of Alexandra Park. 2019. 'Restoring the Park'.
14. Presentation by Elizabeth Knowles during our final workshop on 11 June 2019.
15. Conversation with Elena Besussi, resident in Alexandra and Ainsworth Estate, in June 2019 and her presentation in our final workshop on 11 June 2019.
16. Elizabeth Hopkirk. 2019. 'Council Works "vandalising" Neave Brown's Masterpiece', *Building Design* (12 July 2019). https://www.bdonline.co.uk/news/council-works-vandalising-neave-browns-masterpiece/5100578.article. Accessed 27 July 2019.
17. Elizabeth Hopkirk. 2019. 'Camden Brings in Levitt Bernstein to Protect Alexandra Road', *Building Design* (26 July 2019). https://www.bdonline.co.uk/news/camden-brings-in-levitt-bernstein-to-protect-alexandra-road/5100804.article#.XTq_9ORF6pc.twitter. Accessed 27 July 2019.
18. Conversation with Elena Besussi, resident in Alexandra and Ainsworth Estate, in June 2019 and her presentation in our final workshop on 11 June 2019.
19. Historic England. 2019. 'How To Get Historic Buildings or Sites Protected Through Listing'. https://historicengland.org.uk/listing/apply-for-listing/. Accessed 28 July 2019.

Part II
Tools for Community-Led Regeneration

From the case studies discussed in Part I, we have identified a set of tools, strategies and actions that residents resisting demolition and/or proposing community-led plans have used. The tools have different objectives and also respond to different degrees of participation, ranging from full community control to exerting influence on the decision-making process. They also include both formal planning tools and other tools, actions and strategies outside planning.

We have organised the examination of these tools into five chapters: 'Gaining residents' control', 'Localism Act 2011', 'Policies for community participation in regeneration', 'Using the law and challenging redevelopment through the courts' and 'Informal tools and strategies'. Chapter 8, 'Gaining residents' control', explains mechanisms by which residents can gain control over the ownership (Right to Transfer) and over the repairs and maintenance (Right to Manage) of their estate. Chapter 9, 'Localism Act 2011', discusses the planning frameworks introduced by the Localism Act to provide communities with planning frameworks through which they can shape the policies for the future development of their neighbourhoods. Chapter 10, 'Policies for community participation in regeneration', describes the available national and London policies for participating in decisions on the future of their neighbourhoods. Chapter 11, 'Using the law and challenging redevelopment through the courts', explains how and when to bring the council to Judicial Review on the grounds of failing in their public equality duty under the Equality Act 2010 or not carrying out a lawful consultation. Finally, chapter 12, 'Informal tools and strategies', considers the tools, strategies and actions that exist outside planning. It first explains the usefulness of putting together a People's Plan (also named community plan or community-led plan by some groups) and then describes some of the campaigning strategies used in the case studies.

There is a specific London context for all of the tools explored in this part of the book. However, despite the London specificity, these tools are also applicable to the rest of the UK, and indeed to a global context. Policy vehicles, such as the London Plan and the Mayor's Housing Strategy, are relevant not only in terms of how they were put together as strategic documents, but also – more importantly from this work's perspective – in showing what the avenues for community involvement were before, during and after consultation.

In addition, other metropolitan, city-region and unitary authorities are having to develop strategic plans across England and the whole of the UK. They are also having to respond to demands for community participation. There are some emerging examples of strategic plans for city-regions on the level that the London Plan has, such as the Liverpool City Region Spatial Development Strategy and Greater Manchester Spatial Framework. It is not clear to what extent these are accompanied by coordinated community consultations on a scale seen in the London Plan, for example. Therefore, London is not an exception nor just a relic from the regional tier of planning otherwise abolished in 2010. Instead, it can in some ways be seen as a precursor. This is especially true in the ways in which community networks have coordinated to be involved in, submit evidence to and to a small extent shape the strategic plan for London, through a range of tools – as explored in the case studies in Part I.

The case studies have shown that the key is not to employ *one* of these strategies, but rather a combination of them. We have explained when we recommend the use of these strategies and the difficulties communities may find. We have then supplied advice on how to overcome those difficulties and where financial or technical support can be found, citing examples in the relevant case studies. To get the most from this toolkit, we recommend looking both at the tools themselves and at how the case studies have used them.

8
Gaining residents' control

There are a range of ways in which residents can take some control when faced with processes of regeneration, demolition and potential displacement. Consultation is often guided by pre-established priorities of the local authorities or developers involved. These same local authorities, however, have to abide by formal planning legislation, including the range of Rights, including the Right to Manage (RtM) and the Right to Transfer (RtT), as well as the newer Rights established within the Localism Act 2011 (see chapter 9). Although some of these tools have not been fully tested, they allow for a range of potential control – from full ownership and management through to control over the creation or involvement in making plans and the processes involved in regeneration. The tools offer residents the means to move from a position of being subjects of plans to a position in which they have more power and agency over the proposed changes and processes that affect their collective lives.

These legal frameworks are still being tested across London. Groups such as West Ken Gibbs Green Community Homes (chapter 2) and Cressingham Gardens Community (chapter 3) have been looking at how they can apply the legislation in their own cases and to suit their own particular circumstances. All these groups are in the middle of lengthy disputes with local authorities and developers. They are also witnesses to the changes in their areas in terms of tenure mix, changes to maintenance regimes and the effects of long-term under-investment. The level of residents' involvement in their respective campaigns has varied. In some cases core groups have had support workers shaping their campaigns; other times groups have relied purely on voluntary work. The gaining of resident control through the use of these tools therefore needs to be measured against not only the constraints facing the people involved but also the resources available and the time frames.

Regarding the people involved, there needs to be support of the community and of a majority of residents. There is usually a core group of workers at the heart of a campaign, who are representative of wider resident interests and who try to articulate these interests in the best ways that they can, while faced with the potential divisions, acrimony and even burn-out that can often accompany lengthy campaigns. At the same time, however, valuable skills are developed by all people involved. These include managing meetings, organising themselves, facilitating discussions and galvanising support from both within and beyond the community under pressure from regeneration plans.

The avenues to gain greater control depend on the resources available to residents, which include a knowledge of tools, campaigning tactics and organising strategies. Access to funding is important to pay for the completion of relevant studies, the hire of equipment and professional services, or to purchase materials needed for campaigning and developing the documentation needed for implementing any of the Rights discussed below. Finally, it is worth considering the time dimension – not only in terms of the time required for implementing any of these Rights, but also the need for appropriate timing of the activities involved (i.e. 'good timing'). The Rights can be used as a strategic tool within a wider campaign to gain more resident control. Exercising these Rights brings people together within the community; it can also involve people from beyond the area who bring their own interests, skills and resources. Even when such campaigns are not successful, they can result in lasting achievements such as creating stronger groups, increasing individual and collective knowledge, and broadening awareness and solidarity with a particular campaign or issue.

While the timing and resourcing to exercise the Rights, both to Manage and to Transfer, might be similar, their goals can also be pursued in parallel, as some of the cases attest. However, it is useful to examine the differences in the Rights, both in terms of possible concrete outcomes of the form of control achieved(RtM) if the group is successful, and also through the processes needed. The Right to Manage can be seen as a step towards greater control by residents, and the establishment of a Tenant Management Organisation (TMO) is a good indicator of organisational skills and of governance learning for groups pursuing greater resident control. Both the RtM and the establishment of a TMO enable a group to develop a different working relationship with local authorities; the process may also draw divided groups together. The Right to Transfer is a further step in gaining resident control; it will eventually require a range of new knowledge, more resources and a longer time frame.

It is useful to frame these Rights within the framework of Arnstein's ladder of participation (see fig. C.1 in 'Conclusions'). Here we can start to break down what the top rungs of the ladder represent within the category of 'degrees of citizen power'.[1] Moving upwards, the top three rungs represent partnership, delegated power and citizen control. The Right to Manage can be classified as a delegated power as well as allowing residents to have greater control as citizens over questions of maintenance and management of their homes. The Right to Transfer is situated further up the ladder, a point at which resident control becomes a reality through legal ownership. The ladder frames the ways in which forms of participation can increase resident control over their housing and planning more generally. It provides a valuable visual tool to show both how residents can find ways to move up the 'rungs' or to select the right 'rung' for their needs; each individual 'rung' has its range of tools and strategies which can be used to acquire more control.[2]

In the following sections we cover both the Right to Manage and the Right to Transfer. The former came out of the Housing Act 1985, supporting the set-up of Tenant Management Organisations. The Right to Transfer, modelled on the Right to Manage, can also be seen as part of the broad efforts to demunicipalise the provision of housing during the 1980s. The Right to Transfer is related to what was previously the Right to Acquire or, to use its political name, 'Tenants' Choice'. Walterton and Elgin Community Homes (WECH) (see chapter 1) used 'Tenants' Choice' legislation to force the local authority to dispose of stock to a community-owned housing association, despite the legislation having been relatively untested across the country. Indeed, it remained on the statute book for around seven years, and was then amended so that only an approved landlord could use the legislation and the process would be subject to a ballot by residents.[3] There is, therefore, a legislative relationship between the Right to Manage, the Right to Acquire (or Tenants' Choice) and the Right to Transfer, which we will trace in the following pages.

Right to Manage

Type of tool	Planning legislation
National, GLA or Local level	National
Act, year	Commonhold and Leasehold Reform Act 2002 Localism Act 2011
Regulations, year	The Housing (Right to Manage) Regulations 2012[4] The Housing (Right to Manage) Regulations 2008[5] The Housing (Right to Manage) Regulations 1994[6]
Guidance	

Description of Right to Manage

The Right to Manage (RtM) is the right for both tenants and leaseholders of a building, or indeed an estate containing flats, to take over management of the building(s) from the freeholder, using an RtM company.

The Right to Manage has given council tenants a collective right to take over the management of the council housing where they live. This can occur when a local tenant group believes that they could provide a better or more cost-effective service, such as arranging repairs or estate cleaning, if they were to have direct control of the funds that the council spends on that service. When tenants join together to manage their own homes, they need to set up a Tenant Management Organisation (TMO). TMOs have been managing council housing around the country for nearly 50 years, with such arrangements now extending from council-owned properties managed by a TMO to private leaseholders.[7]

The legislation itself has evolved from the introduction of the Housing (Rents and Subsidies) Act 1975. This enabled local authorities to delegate budgets and responsibility for housing management and maintenance to TMOs. Under the Labour government of the time, Tenant Management Co-operatives were set up and, subsequently, section 27AB of the Housing Act 1985 allowed councils to hand over management of estates to these Tenant Management Co-operatives.[8] The 1986 Housing and Planning Act further provided powers to grant funding to tenant groups for advice and support, in order that they could develop TMOs. In 1987 the Estate Management Board model of TMOs was developed as part of the Priority Estates Project and Estate Action.

With the Housing (Right to Manage) Regulations 1994, powers were introduced for TMOs to enable residents of council housing or housing association homes in the UK to take over responsibility for the running of their homes.[9] The Commonhold and Leasehold Reform Act 2002 extended this right to leaseholders to acquire the landlord's management functions by transfer to a company set up by them – a Right to Manage (RtM) company – which applied to private leaseholders, as opposed to council tenants.[10]

In 2002 an independent evaluation of TMOs was commissioned by the Office of the Deputy Prime Minister (ODPM). It led to the 2008 Right to Manage amendments that introduced voluntary agreements and simplified the process to one ballot. In 2008 Local Management Agreements introduced voluntary agreements for self-management on a small scale; these were followed in 2012 by new Right to Manage regulations, intended to simplify the system.[11] The various stages of legislation – 1975, 1985, 1986 and 1994 – all seemed to have had the establishment or strengthening of TMOs as their objectives. These progressive developments have to be seen in the context of wider dynamics in housing policy – including the attempts by successive political regimes to diversify social housing provision, but often also to support the demunicipalisation of social housing.

Usefulness for community-led social housing regeneration

Right to Manage allows for the creation of community-based, co-operatively run, representative and local organisations that collectively ensure the management quality of housing. There are now over 200 TMOs working as community groups and improving conditions of both the physical and social infrastructures in their estates or buildings. Management agreements are negotiated with the landlord to take on limited, local responsibilities financed from the rental revenue. The Right to Manage has been supported by governments of all parties since the 1980s. They have funded training and given advice to groups wishing to pursue the Right to Manage.

The RtM legislation and process can also serve to support community-led social housing regeneration, enabling such social housing groups to take a lead in developing their own public realm, investing in their homes and developing plans for their estates. In addition, using the Right to Transfer (see below), TMOs now have the opportunity, in theory, to move from management to ownership, retaining proven structures such as the TMOs for running their housing.

A report on TMOs found that:

> Between 1991 and 1997 the formation rate rose to an average 13 or 14 TMOs per year. The rate of new formation slowed down after 1997, averaging 4 per year in the last decade. Information about closures of TMOs is very patchy, but there are some indications that TMOs closure rates in the last decade are either roughly the same or slightly higher than the rate of new TMOs being formed.[12]

To set up a Tenant Management Organisation, tenants enter into a legal agreement with their landlord to carry out such specific housing management functions as caretaking, rent collection and repairs. The number of housing management functions that TMOs take over can vary, with many taking on increased responsibilities over time.

There are three main stages in setting up a TMO: the first is development and feasibility; the second is the ballot of tenants; and the third is creating a management agreement. The last includes a competence assessment, carried out by an independent assessor. All TMOs are legally recognised organisations and take different forms. Some are Tenant Management Co-operatives, while others take the form of not-for-profit companies. Some TMOs (the co-operative model) have resident-only Boards. Another common model consists of resident-majority Boards, where places are allocated on the Board for council staff, councillors and others (Estate Management Boards). All tenants of homes managed by TMOs must be able to become members, and the majority of Directors must be elected by TMO members.[13]

On 6 August 2012, following extensive consultation with the wider housing sector, a replacement set of Right to Manage regulations, designed to provide a more straightforward procedure, came into force. Under the Housing (Right to Manage) (England) Regulations 2012,[14] these apply to England only. These new regulations ensured that TMOs could now use the RtT regulations, in theory, to move from management as a TMO to ownership, retaining the proven structures for running their council estates. Although they may have sufficient resources to cover part or all of the costs of the transfer process, they still would face a major challenge if they wish to create a stand-alone, community-owned, resident-controlled Private Registered Provider of social housing, as outlined in the RtT legislation.[15]

Difficulties found in the context of community-led social housing regeneration

Tenants need to have received appropriate training and have sufficient time available to be able to take on the tasks of management, oversight of contracts and delivery of services. These tasks may also involve handling budgets, issues of staff employment and ensuring service standards. While there are challenges facing governance, they can be overcome with experience, resources and support. To this end, groups usually employ professional staff; it is rare for the main responsibilities to be carried out by volunteers.

The actual use of Right to Manage has declined in recent years among estate residents. It has instead become more common in the private sector among leaseholders from private landlords. Nonetheless, it is still an important tool for groups to use, although one difficulty is dealing with areas of mixed tenures. In extreme cases, these may include councils outsourcing their social housing rentals through large private rental companies, sitting alongside both short-term private social tenants and also sub-tenants and renters from leaseholders. This kind of situation makes establishing who is eligible for balloting or involvement in the process of setting up the RtM very difficult.

Another issue has arisen after the Grenfell fire in North Kensington that occurred in June 2017. It relates to the role that the Kensington and Chelsea TMO had in the management of social housing across the borough. Originally set up to provide management services for council housing across the whole borough, it was in reality more of an Arm's Length Management Organisation – too large and with serious governance problems, partly caused because it was not community-based. These lessons were learned at a heavy and tragic cost of human life.[16]

When we recommend to use this tool

It is clear from the case studies discussed above that this tool can be recommended in situations where residents have felt that the local authority or organisation responsible for managing repairs and maintenance has not been doing an effective or efficient job. In the case of Cressingham Gardens, for example, there has been long-term under-investment and systemic failures in the management of maintenance contracts. This has resulted in shoddy work that sometimes even damaged the integrity of the estate's character and made conditions more dangerous, such as the resurfacing of the steps or works to the guttering systems, which were both badly carried out. When residents are seeking better control of repairs, maintenance work and other service contracts then the Right to Manage can be very useful.

This tool could also be used as part of a longer-term campaign to take more control of the management of an estate. Residents can begin to organise and use the Right to Manage tool as a means to bring people from across different tenures together. By initiating the conversations and governance discussions needed to pursue a more active role in management, residents are able to come together, perhaps with a longer-term vision that could focus on preventing the demolition of the estate. This could then move on to developing propositions for their own project of refurbishment and improvement of the physical and social infrastructures of their homes and their estates collectively.

Technical and financial support available

The most up-to-date information for groups needing support as a Tenant Management Organisation, as well as for groups who want to exercise the Right to Manage, is available from the National Federation of Tenant Management Organisations (NFTMO).[17] This has extensive and free resources including directory listing for funding organisations, support services, housing organisations, employment support and tenant participation advice, as well as a range of contacts of other well-established groups around the country. Other useful resources for groups available from the NFTMO include a business planning guide for TMOs to prepare community-focused business plans, and guides for practical ways in which groups can keep in touch with tenants and members. The material included is a useful toolkit for staying in touch, improving the governance and management of a group, providing an effective housing service and guiding people on how to get advice and support for the Right to Manage process.[18] The latter material includes useful information on balloting, calculating allowances and managing relationships with local authorities, together with the statutory guidance from government.

Another useful tool is the common assessment model standards (2012) – the set of standards that groups must meet before a TMO can be recognised. These 17 standards are grouped under the headings of: realistic and viable aims, good levels of communication and organisation among residents, demonstrations of good functioning and control, and demonstrating the provision of an effective housing service.[19] Finally the NFTMO also has a service for identifying an adviser for the set-up of a Tenant Management Organisation, the development of a Local Management Agreement and exploring the option of a Tenant Led Stock Transfer. In terms of financial support, another avenue is through the Tenant Services Authority's National Tenant Empowerment Programme, which provides grants to fund training and support for TMOs.

Case studies

One of the most recent successes from the cases we have explored in the first part of the book is that of Cressingham Gardens (chapter 3). Here the residents, as part of their broader campaign to prevent the demolition of their estate and gain more control, chose to use the Right to Manage legislation. The estate residents had been suffering for many years from the long-term under-investment and poor maintenance services provided by the council. After contesting the quality and costs of the ongoing maintenance and repair programme through a series of in-depth analyses, using Freedom of Information requests, of contractual costs and spends by the local authority, the group was successful in transferring the management of estate repairs from the council to a community-owned company. This was achieved after having given notice for the Right to Manage and pursuing an estate-wide ballot on the decision. The Right to Manage request was successful.[20]

Right to Transfer

Type of tool	Planning framework
National, GLA or Local level	National
Act, year	Housing Act 1985 (as amended by section 34a)
Regulations, year	Housing and Regeneration Act 2008 section 296 Housing (Right to Transfer from a Local Authority Landlord) (England) Regulations 2013
Guidance	Giving Tenants Control: Right to Transfer and Right to Manage Regulations Consultation 2012 Housing Transfer Manual 2014
See also:	Tenants' Choice legislation 1988 (repealed and superseded)

Description of Right to Transfer

The Right to Transfer (RtT) is a legal framework[21] that enables council tenants to change their landlord through the collective transfer of ownership of their homes to a private registered provider of social housing of their choice.[22] In effect, it forces local authorities to transfer their housing stock to a new landlord chosen by residents. The new landlord, which could in theory be a tenant-run organisation or partnership, would have to pay the value of stock (the Transfer Value) to the council and commit to the development of the local community through additional investment for the refurbishment of current housing and the supply of more (see the possibility of debt write-off for transfers of more than 500 homes below).

The Right to Transfer legislation is an amendment of section 34A of the Housing Act 1985 through the introduction of section 296 of the Housing and Regeneration Act 2008. It grants secure council tenants the right to require a council to co-operate with a transfer proposal for a minimum of 100 houses let under secure tenancies within a contiguous transfer area.

The Notice of Proposal is prepared by the tenant group and submitted to the local authority expressing the tenant group's interest in pursuing housing stock transfer. Once the proposal notice is accepted, a Feasibility Study is carried out, examining the options for transfer and costs. This must confirm the houses to be transferred and agree that these are the same houses originally identified in the proposal notice. The study should also specify and provide an assessment of options for transfer, including no change. The financial viability must include condition of the houses, future maintenance and repair costs, the projected level of rental income and leaseholder service charges.

If the study is accepted by the local authority, the process then moves to the Development stage. This sets out the timetable, identifies new landlords and provides a business case to the GLA (if in London) and to the government, including a request for funding of debt write-off if needed. Once the business case is approved by the GLA or government, a consultation and ballot with tenants is held. If this is successful, consent is sought from the Secretary of State. If approved, the transfer should theoretically occur during the following 6 to 12 months.

Usefulness for community-led social housing regeneration

In theory, when council-led regeneration involves the demolition and displacement of people, the RtT can be a way for tenants to protect their social housing. The legislation was drafted so that tenants would find it easier to take a lead locally for their housing, either by taking over responsibility for managing housing services (through the Right to Manage) or by exploring options for transfer from their local authority (Right to Transfer). The latter offers a way in which a group of tenants seeking to 'explore the benefits of a change of landlord ... can transfer ownership of those homes to a private registered provider of social housing'.[23]

The tenant group must demonstrate local support, including a minimum of 20 per cent of the secure tenants and 20 per cent of leaseholders of the houses in the area proposed for transfer. In this way the tenants in the proposed area can change their landlord and, in addition, propose a different solution for the ownership and management of their homes. This can lead to greater control of maintenance contracts and standards, finances, the governance of housing management and the development of new houses.

Once the transfer has been achieved, the new organisation can then refurbish the houses to the standards that the tenants demand. Having a smaller organisation enables greater accountability and more direct democratic control over the governance of the management of housing management. Greater control has also been found to increase the levels of wellbeing among tenants;[24] they feel more empowered to get involved and participate in the process of regeneration.[25] For example, residents have more control over the revenue from rents, which can go directly to repairs and property management, and over contract agreements, including rents, tenures and service contractors. The tenant group would have either to set up as a community-led private registered provider of social housing or to join an existing private registered provider, such as a housing association.

Difficulties found in the context of community-led social housing regeneration

The legislation as it stands is relatively complex and ill-defined. It has a number of practical difficulties due to the number of steps involved, the time required and the need for robust evidence in support of each test of opinion, requiring professional inputs. Most estates now have a range of housing tenures and the tenants may have a range of opinions and choices, potentially leading to difficulties in organising residents. The support and cross-tenure collaboration of both tenants and leaseholders is needed in most cases, as tenures of households on estates now tend to be mixed. They often include private rented tenants and sub-tenants, as well as having multi-occupancy of houses or temporary occupants. The different groups would have a range of opinions on council-led services, making any concerted approach more difficult without some form of community organising.

The transfer of social housing and community-led regeneration will only be achieved if the business case is approved, together with appropriate levels of financing, presumably from private sector or grant funding. There is potential support for debt write-off, which requires approval from the local authority, but this is provided to support large-scale transfers (of more than 500 homes) dependent on the approval of a business plan; it is not intended for small-scale transfers.[26]

The labyrinthine process will test the most committed of communities. Problems can be exacerbated by the arbitrary behaviour of a local authority, coupled with a lack of professional support or financial resources. An example is the inclusion of four tests of tenant opinion, making it a laborious and time-consuming endeavour, which furthermore requires considerable input from professionals as well as the co-operation of the local authority who are obliged to conduct a fair ballot as part of their formal consultation.

The organisation to which the houses are transferred would be either a community-led provider or an existing social housing registered provider. However, it is more likely to be an existing housing association. This requires a competitive or best-value process with, in either case, allowance for a long lead-in time. The assets could, in theory, be transferred to a community-led provider, such as a trust established by the tenant group with support from a larger housing entity. In the case of a new, community-led provider, the council is unlikely to approve the stock transfer to a newly formed housing organisation unless it can demonstrate that it is professionally managed or supported, well-staffed and resourced, and has the capacity and experience to manage the housing refurbishment, management and development. There is consequently a risk that even though, in principle, the legislation provides a community-led tool for housing control, it would not be successful. It is not conceived as a tool for overall community control, but rather as a process for the privatisation of housing stock enabled by tenants as part of an estate regeneration strategy.

Finally, it is clear that the local authority can block the transfer and has many opportunities to do so throughout the RtT process, as does the Homes and Communities Agency, GLA and/or government. Although this may be challenged through a Judicial Review, the recent reforms to legal aid have made this harder and would require yet more financial resources and even stronger commitments from the community (see section on Judicial Reviews in chapter 11). It would be easy, for example, for the local authority to seek an unfavourable determination on the request to exercise the RtT and not to co-operate. Therefore the power imbalance between the under-funded tenant group and the relatively well-resourced local authority can remain unaddressed. The finite and limited resources available to the tenant group are compounded by the ability of the local authority to control the timetable of transfer. These points are exacerbated in situations when the RtT is sought urgently or where tenant groups have the most incentive to use the legislation, such as when they are facing unwanted regeneration plans.

When we recommend to use this tool

The RtT can be seen as part of a longer process of residents gaining more direct control of their own homes on a trajectory that may start from exercising the Right to Manage. Residents can use the RtT not only when they are threatened by housing demolition and regeneration plans, but also beforehand, to protect their homes and take greater control. However, both instances require organisation and the existence of a strong TMO, Tenants and Residents Association (TRA) or local resident group of some kind.

The recent determinations regarding both Cressingham Gardens[27] and West Ken Gibbs Green Community Homes (WKGGCH)[28] from the Secretary of State have made it clear that an important factor which is taken into consideration is whether the Right to Transfer is detrimental for the regeneration plans of the area. In the case of Cressingham Gardens, where the RtT has been allowed to go ahead despite the local authority's opposition, Lambeth Council was unable to demonstrate that it would be detrimental. This was mainly because they had not made much progress with their masterplan and were only delivering 120 more homes than the People's Plan, considered by the Secretary of State to be insignificant compared to the overall local authority numbers.

In the case of WKGGCH, the estate is part of a larger contiguous Opportunity Area and the large, although currently stalled, regeneration scheme of Earl's Court. Here there are plans for the provision of thousands of homes (see chapter 2). The council, in this case, thought it had sufficient grounds to demonstrate that it would impact the regeneration of the area since removing the estates from the Earl's Court Masterplan would, in their view, compromise the whole scheme. However, in the rebuttal of the July 2019 decision, WKGGCH states that it had been proven in its submission to exercise the RtT that the demolition of the estates will not happen as planned, and indeed the planners and landowners had adopted a policy to exclude the West Kensington and Gibbs Green estates from the wider Earl's Court Masterplan. Discussions had in fact taken place with the planning authorities to increase the density on other parts of the Opportunity Area in order to maintain the density of new housing over the whole site for which they were aiming.[29]

Under Right to Transfer regulations, the local authority can apply to the Secretary of State to determine whether the proposed transfer of houses 'set out in the proposal notice will have a significant detrimental effect on the provision of housing services … or the regeneration of the area'.[30] Both points are important to bear in mind when considering how to use the regulations and the timing of their use. The resident group will need to evaluate the size of the area for which they would like to seek a Right to Transfer, and also consider the context within which they are exercising the Right to Transfer – in terms of both ongoing regeneration plans and in ensuring that their plans for a community – or resident-led regeneration programme are not thwarted. Of course, the irony here is that regeneration is often the inspiration for council tenants to consider exercising the RtT in order to have a landlord of their own choice:

> By excluding estates which are the subject of 'regeneration', the Government is denying the RtT to the very Tenant Groups who are most motivated and most likely to achieve successful transfer. The predisposition that the Council's proposed scheme is necessarily better than the Tenant Group's scheme is doubly ironic since most 'regeneration' schemes involve at least an element of housing stock transfer.[31]

It is therefore essential to build up a case with evidence, plans and proposals in place to pre-empt these arguments being used against the residents involved.

Technical and financial support available

A range of support is available from external organisations providing organisational, technical and financial support. However, as we have seen from the cases presented in Part I of this book, many skills develop as part of a group's own campaigning and organising activities. Some specialised skills might include maintenance audits,[32] balloting of residents, campaigning and community organising, for example, while technical skills such as preparing valuation and feasibility studies, developing of business cases, developing architectural plans,[33] and understanding planning tools and legislation have been acquired by some groups. This may be because of professional expertise among the group members, or through voluntary support from external individuals or organisations, or through professional support funded by crowdfunding and other funding sources, or by funded support from umbrella organisations, such as Locality.

In terms of financial support, specific grants are available for groups to develop their plans and documents needed for Right to Transfer applications and to receive advice on the specific process. One grant is from Locality; other organisations offer qualitative research skills as well as campaign support and community organising, all required as part of the wider effort leading to the use of RtT. In particular, similar to the way that Right to Manage implies the development of institutions within the community, RtT needs effective organisations run by residents. These must be able to support the longer-term planning needed to manage and take ownership of the estate, such as TRAs and other resident neighbourhood or community groups. The support that can be given to TMOs, for example, can include training and strategy development. This will encourage the group to think strategically about the Right to Transfer and to develop the necessary skills and partnerships to manage contracts, business planning, management and maintenance – as well as the often-overlooked area of developing governance within groups.

One important organisation willing to help support the establishment of new Community Land Trusts, which can be a form of owning the housing stock under RtT, is the Community-led Housing Hub at regional level. The hub in London,[34] for example, has been developing links both with groups interested in new build or self-build and with those interested in setting up partnerships or legal entities of their own to manage and own their housing. There has therefore been substantial progress in recent years at a policy level, and with funding support from both the GLA and central government for community-led housing.

Where communities are bringing forward proposals that are broadly in line with the ambitions of the government, GLA or local authority, they are thus finding the level of professional support and funding they need. Most of the case studies, however, are pursuing plans that challenge or resist proposals and developments; they may promote ideas that do not follow their local authorities' plans. However, the community-led housing sector does need to think strategically about how they should support such oppositional campaigns. One option may be to provide support in ways that help them move beyond the oppositional to the propositional. This is an approach that most of the case studies have achieved.

Case studies

There are very few cases of groups that have used the Right to Transfer regulations and, at present, none of these have been successful. WECH was successful under the forerunner of this piece of legislation, and their story sets an important precedent (see chapter 1).

A notable historical case is the Friday Hill Tenant Management Organisation (TMO) in Waltham Forest, which used the RtT after forming as a TMO in 1998. The council stalled the process, but did offer the group greater autonomy and funding. This was deemed a success in terms of using the RtT as a negotiation tool or campaigning tool to gain greater control.

WKGGCH has been battling against the large-scale regeneration of the area as part of the Earl's Court development led by the private sector (see chapter 2). They have used the RtT, but found it time-consuming because of tenure splits and uncertainty of the council's position. While there are also many people in favour, they are not necessarily registered secure tenants. The group has had legal advice from solicitors and support from trade unions, as well as funding from foundations. However, the council has been working closely with developers and has indicated that the default position will be a rejection of the transfer proposal, without strong evidence against it. After almost three years since they submitted their request to the Secretary of State, the RtT was not recommended on the basis of the council's submissions, although WKGGCH are considering challenging this decision.[35]

Cressingham Gardens Community, in Lambeth, believed that the use of the RtT process could be a means of protecting and challenging the demolition plans as imposed on them by Lambeth Council. The process was within a lengthy and contentious campaign that included two Judicial Reviews and the preparation of an alternative People's Plan under the campaign of Save Cressingham Gardens (see chapter 3). Again, the default position of the local authority was to reject any transfer proposals, despite some evidence to suggest that alternative plans could be feasible – and indeed more desirable for the current residents. The RtT was given the go-ahead by the Secretary of State on 9 July 2019. In any case, the success of Cressingham Gardens and of the Cressingham Gardens Community (CGC) is notable at this stage. It provides both a remarkable case study and a precedent for other residents in their attempts to secure greater control of their estate and of their homes.

Notes

1. Sherry Phyllis Arnstein. 1969. 'A Ladder of Citizen Participation', *Journal of the American Planning Association* 35(4): 216–24.
2. See recent double issue of *Built Environment* (45.1 and 45.2) entitled 'Outlooks on Participating: People, Plans & Places' (Lucy Natarajan. 2019. 'Outlooks on Participating', *Built Environment* 45(1): 5–6) marking 50 years since Arnstein's eponymous ladder of participation.
3. In interview with Jonathan Rosenberg (WECH) and Zoe Savory (WKGGCH) on 17 November 2017.
4. 'The Housing (Right to Manage) (England) Regulations 2012'. http://www.legislation.gov.uk/uksi/2012/1821/contents/made. Accessed 28 July 2019.
5. 'The Housing (Right to Manage) (England) Regulations 2008'. http://www.legislation.gov.uk/uksi/2008/2361/contents/made. Accessed 28 July 2019.
6. 'The Housing (Right to Manage) Regulations 1994'. http://www.legislation.gov.uk/uksi/1994/627/contents/made. Accessed 28 July 2019.
7. See the website of the National Federation of Tenant Management Organisations. http://www.nftmo.co.uk. Accessed 28 July 2019.
8. 'Housing Act 1985: Management Agreements with Tenant Management Organisations'. https://www.legislation.gov.uk/ukpga/1985/68/section/27AB. Accessed 27 July 2019.

9. 'The Housing (Right to Manage) Regulations 1994'.
10. See Anne Power and Rebecca Tunstall. 1995. *Swimming Against the Tide: Polarisation or Progress on 20 Unpopular Council Estates, 1980–1995*. Joseph Rowntree Foundation: York.
11. Rachel Newton and Rebecca Tunstall. 2012. *Lessons for Localism: Tenant Self-Management*. London: Urban Forum.
12. Newton and Tunstall. 2012. *Lessons for Localism: Tenant Self-Management*, 15.
13. Newton and Tunstall. 2012. *Lessons for Localism: Tenant Self-Management*.
14. 'The Housing (Right to Manage) (England) Regulations 2012'.
15. Jonathan Rosenberg. 2013. *Widening the Door to Community Ownership – Right to Transfer: S34A Housing Act 1985 – Challenges and Opportunities*, 17. Self-published report..
16. See the introduction to the in-depth study of social housing by Stuart Hodkinson. 2019. *Safe as Houses: Private Greed, Political Negligence and Housing Policy After Grenfell*. Manchester: Manchester University Press.
17. National Federation of Tenant Management Organisations. https://www.nftmo.co.uk. Accessed 27 July 2019.
18. 'Toolbox of the National Federation of Tenant Management Organisations'. http://www.nftmo.co.uk/content/content_toolbox.html. Accessed 27 July 2019.
19. 'Streamlined Common Assessment Model Standards 2012'. http://www.nftmo.co.uk/numo_img/library/Streamlined_CAM_Standards_2012.pdf. Accessed 27 July 2019.
20. See chapter 3 on Cressingham Gardens Community and the Save Cressingham campaign, also chronicled here: https://savecressingham.wordpress.com. Accessed 27 July 2019.
21. Ministry of Housing, Communities and Local Government. 'Housing (Right to Transfer from a Local Authority Landlord) (England) Regulations 2013'. https://www.gov.uk/government/uploads/system/uploads/attachment_data/file/256523/The_Housing__Right_To_Transfer_from_A_Local_Authority_Landlord___England__Regulations_2013.pdf. Accessed 27 July 2019.
22. This section builds on work done by a group of students looking at the potential for Right to Transfer for a community group during the MSc module 'From Strategic Vision to Urban Plan' at The Bartlett School of Planning, UCL. The course was coordinated by Elena Besussi and Daniel Fitzpatrick. The students' report looked at the process of exercising the Right to Buy and case studies included West Ken Gibbs Green and Friday Hill Tenant Management Organisation, among others.
23. Ministry of Housing, Communities and Local Government, 'Housing (Right to Transfer from a Local Authority Landlord) (England) Regulations 2013', 4.
24. Peter Ambrose and Julia Stone. 2010. *Happiness, Heaven and Hell in Paddington: A Comparative Study of the Empowering Management Practices of WECH*. Brighton: University of Sussex.
25. Madhu Satsangi and Susan Murray. 2011. *Community Empowerment. Final Report to Walterton and Elgin Community Homes*. Stirling: University of Stirling.
26. Ministry of Housing, Communities and Local Government, 'Housing (Right to Transfer from a Local Authority Landlord) (England) Regulations 2013', 11.
27. Ministry of Housing, Communities and Local Government. 'Right to Transfer Determination: Cressingham Gardens Estate, 9 July 2019'. https://assets.publishing.service.gov.uk/government/uploads/system/uploads/attachment_data/file/816102/Cressingham_Gardens_determination_letter_Redacted.pdf. Accessed 16 July 2019.
28. 'Right to Transfer Determinations: West Kensington and Gibbs Green Estates, 9 July 2019'. https://assets.publishing.service.gov.uk/government/uploads/system/uploads/attachment_data/file/816103/West_Ken_Gibbs_Green_determination_letter_Redacted.pdf. Accessed 16 July 2019.
29. Correspondence with Jonathan Rosenberg (community organiser of WKGGCH), 25 July 2019.
30. Ministry of Housing, Communities and Local Government. 'Housing (Right to Transfer from a Local Authority Landlord) (England) Regulations 2013'.
31. Jonathan Rosenberg. 2013. *Widening the Door to Community Ownership – Right to Transfer: S34A Housing Act 1985 – Challenges and Opportunities*, 20.
32. See the work of data and housing scholar-activist Tom Keene. http://db-estate.co.uk/. Accessed 27 July 2019.
33. See the work of Architects for Social Housing on WKGG or of the architect Ashvin de Vos of Variant Office on Cressingham Gardens.
34. Community-led Housing London: Resource and advice hub. https://www.communityledhousing.london. Accessed 29 July 2019.
35. Correspondence with Jonathan Rosenberg, community organiser from WKGGCH, 25 July 2019.

9
Localism Act 2011

The Localism Act was introduced in 2011 with the aim of devolving decision-making power to local communities. It introduced a series of planning frameworks that communities can use to shape planning policies in their local area, to undertake developments, to identify their community assets and to be able to bid for them if and when these assets are sold. Some years after its implementation, many doubts still remain about its effectiveness and capacity to empower communities, especially in urban areas.[1]

In this chapter, we have listed the tools and planning frameworks offered by the Localism Act 2011 that can be used for community-led social housing regeneration, recommended when to use them and how to access financial and technical support. We have also considered the difficulties that communities might face in the process and suggested how to solve them. A large proportion of the chapter is dedicated to the Neighbourhood Plan, since this is one of the main novelties of the Localism Act. It provides residents with the possibility of putting together their plan for the neighbourhood, making it statutory and shaping future developments.

Neighbourhood planning: Neighbourhood Development Plan

Type of tool	Planning framework
National, GLA or Local level	National
Act, year	Localism Act 2011[2]
Regulations, year	The Neighbourhood Planning (General) Regulations 2012 (with updates and amendments)[3]
Guidance	Guidance Neighbourhood Planning[4]
See also:	Neighbourhood Development Order and Community Right to Build Order

Description of neighbourhood planning

Neighbourhood planning was introduced by the Localism Act 2011 and came into force in April 2012. It includes the Neighbourhood Development Plan (referred to here as the Neighbourhood Plan), Neighbourhood Development Order and Community Right to Build Order. This section focuses on the Neighbourhood Plan, described as a 'community-led planning framework for guiding the future development, regeneration and conservation of an area'.[5]

Process

- Neighbourhood Plans can be prepared by parish/town councils or neighbourhood forums.[6] Parish/town councils need to propose the area of the plan to the local authority for designation. Prospective neighbourhood forums need to apply both for the designation of the neighbourhood area and for the designation of the neighbourhood forum.
- Once designated, organisations have to prepare the Neighbourhood Plan by themselves, with access to professional advice. They will also need to follow certain requirements and conditions. These include, among other things, appropriate publicity, community consultation and engagement in all stages, building up the evidence-based documents and conforming to national and local policy.
- Before submitting the plan to the local authority, it will go through a six-week consultation process. After this consultation an updated plan will be produced, along with a report explaining how the plan has addressed the comments.
- After the consultation and modification, the Neighbourhood Plan will be submitted to the local planning authority, together with other documents that explain the process of its production. The local authority will then check whether the process for producing the Neighbourhood Plan has met the requirements.
- The local authority will publicise the plan for another period of six weeks, after which it will send the plan to independent examination. The independent examiners, who assess whether the plan meets basic conditions such as conformity with national and local policy, will then send a report to the local authority.
- The local authority, based on the report of the independent examiners, can make modifications to the Neighbourhood Plan. These will need to be agreed by the neighbourhood planning body and publicised.

- Once the plan has been through these stages, it will go to referendum. If it passes the referendum with over 50 per cent of the votes, the local authority will bring it into force.
- Once it is brought into force, it becomes a statutory planning document. Planning applications need to be in conformity with the plan.

Implementation and delivery of the plan

The implementation of the plan is currently the least clear stage of neighbourhood planning, since it lies mainly on guiding private development and it is not clear how the community will be involved in it. As the Locality guide points out, the role of neighbourhood forums is to produce the plan; they do not have a formal role in its implementation.[7] For the implementation of certain parts of the plan, community groups could use the Community Right to Build Order.

Part of the infrastructural improvements proposed by the Neighbourhood Plan may be delivered with funds from the Community Infrastructure Levy (CIL). Communities that manage to bring a Neighbourhood Plan into force receive 25 per cent or the CIL arising from developments in their area.[8]

Usefulness for community-led social housing regeneration

Residents and tenants in council estates who would like to propose improvements in their neighbourhood, guide future development and/or carry out a community-led regeneration scheme can use the Neighbourhood Plan as a tool. A group of at least 21 people can apply for the designation of a neighbourhood area and forum, and then follow the process described above. Through the construction of a Neighbourhood Plan, they will be able to write policies, make proposals through site allocation and offer infrastructural proposals.

Neighbourhood planning can be an opportunity for avoiding council-led demolition or the privatisation of social housing, instead proposing alternatives based on refurbishment, infill and diverse kinds of improvements. However, a Neighbourhood Plan needs to be in conformity with the Local Plan: it cannot contradict it. For this reason it is advisable that, if possible, the community also participate in the consultation process of the Local Plan to influence policy at local authority level (see chapter 4 on the Greater Carpenters Neighbourhood Forum).[9] Particular attention needs to be paid to local authority policies on refurbishment vs demolition of existing housing stock, housing provision and strategy, and site allocation for the neighbourhood.

When using neighbourhood planning as a tool for proposing alternative plans to demolition, communities may face difficulties in all stages of the process – from the designation of a neighbourhood forum and its area to the delivery of the plan if it is successful.

Being situated in London makes matters even more difficult. Figures suggest that as of 2017, while over 300 Neighbourhood Plans have reached the referendum stage all across England, only five have reached this stage in London.[10] One of the reasons for this is the fact that London has only one parish council, which means that the success of Neighbourhood Plans depends on the initiative of community groups to come together and apply to be designated as a neighbourhood forum by the local authority.[11] Another hurdle to bringing a Neighbourhood Plan into force is the fact that many local authorities in London still do not engage with neighbourhood planning. According to a study developed by NeighbourhoodPlanners.London in 2017, 19 out of 35 local authorities in London are still operating with pre-2012 Core Strategies rather than with post-2012 Local Plans.[12] The pre-2012 Core Strategies cannot define a framework for neighbourhood planning.

Furthermore, the process of putting together a Neighbourhood Plan requires high levels of self-organisation and commitment by residents; it can be perceived to be a 'burdensome'[13] process. This difficulty can particularly affect council estate residents, since they may have fewer resources than others to carry out this process.

In addition to this, Neighbourhood Plans have to overcome certain difficulties when their main objective is to avoid demolition of social housing and propose alternative plans based on infill densification, improvement of dwellings, community facilities and public spaces. One of the main problems is the fact that Neighbourhood Plans cannot contradict Local Plans. If a Local Plan is proposing to redevelop an area, or it is proposing a very high density of homes on the site of the housing estate, the Neighbourhood Plan cannot propose a lower increase of density. In some cases, local authorities refuse to designate a neighbourhood area – or ask to modify the boundaries of it – if it includes a housing estate for which they already have a regeneration plan.[14]

Lastly, if the Neighbourhood Plan is brought into force, the funding for implementing it depends on the new developments that take place in the area. Currently, central government provides funding for encouraging the creation of the Neighbourhood Plan and for developing it. However, it does not provide funding for delivering the public infrastructure nor for improvements proposed in the Neighbourhood Plan. Instead, communities that manage to bring a Neighbourhood Plan into force receive 25 per cent of the CIL arising from developments in their area.[15] This approach means that the funding for implementing the Neighbourhood Plan is subject to the amount of development that takes place in the area. The Department for Communities and Local Government (DCLG) guidance on CIL does not prescribe a specific process on how this money should be spent. Instead it says that it should be done with community consultation and engagement, involving the neighbourhood forum.[16, 17]

The only case study covered here that has used neighbourhood planning is Greater Carpenters Neighbourhood Forum (GCNF). The group of residents used some specific strategies to overcome these difficulties. First, before setting up a neighbourhood forum and putting together a Neighbourhood Plan, they put together a community plan (see chapter 12); this is not statutory, but it can be done faster than a Neighbourhood Plan. This demonstrated that the residents, local businesses, artists and their supporters had the capacity to put together a plan. Second, at the same time as putting a Neighbourhood Plan together, they also engaged in the consultation process on the Local Plan, managing to influence certain policies that favour refurbishment.[18] Third, GCNF is in a very particular situation, because its landlord, London Borough of Newham (LBN), differs from its planning authority, the London Legacy Development Corporation (LLDC). This means that GCNF was designated by the LLDC, not by LBN, and that all the neighbourhood planning process is done through the LLDC.

When we recommend to use this tool

Neighbourhood planning can take a long time. It requires the community to come together with a common purpose, organise themselves, manage to get designation as a neighbourhood forum, put together the Neighbourhood Plan, go through all of the process described above and finally manage to bring the plan into force. Residents, on many occasions, do not have that much time: redevelopment may be approaching faster. For this reason, although neighbourhood planning can be an effective tool for shaping future developments, we recommend that this tool should be used in conjunction with other tools and strategies.

We strongly recommend that, before taking the neighbourhood planning path, communities should put together a People's Plan (chapter 12) (also known as a community plan or community-led plan by other groups). The main reasons for this are that, first, this will provide the community, in a shorter period of time, with a shared vision on the future of their neighbourhood. Second, all information produced in the People's Plan is useful for then putting together a Neighbourhood Plan, if the group do decide to go down that route. Third, the residents will see their capacity to put together a community-led plan. Fourth, in a People's Plan, the community has stronger control on the timing of putting together the plan and do not have any constraints. In addition to this, as the case study of GCNF has shown, it is important to use these policies together with others, such as engaging in the consultation on the Local Plan.[19]

Technical and financial support available

The Department for Local Government and Communities offers funding for preparing a Neighbourhood Plan. The application process is managed by Locality through their website dedicated to neighbourhood planning.[20] Parish councils, neighbourhood forums and prospective neighbourhood forums are eligible to apply for up to £9,000, with the possibility of applying for an additional £8,000 if the groups meet extra eligibility criteria.

Groups facing complex issues can also apply for technical support, which is provided by consultants working in partnership with Locality. They provide 'support packages' that are determined in a list. Groups can also apply for this support through the neighbourhood planning website mentioned above. This technical support can only be used to fund consultants from the company working in partnership with Locality. To fund its own consultants, the group will have to use grants.

Locality is a network of community-led organisations that promote 'community asset ownership, community enterprise and social action'.[21] It has created a wide variety of resources and tools to help communities to set up Neighbourhood Plans and 'locally owned and led organisations'.[22] Its resources include the website MyCommunity,[23] which provides support for community-led initiatives and a dedicated website giving support on neighbourhood planning.[24] The website provides toolkits and guidance, hosts the application process for support and offers advice. Locality has also created the 'Neighbourhood Plans Road Map Guide', which explains neighbourhood planning step-by-step in a more accessible language.

Cases of community-led social housing regeneration that have used this tool

The only council estate that has elaborated a Neighbourhood Plan with the objective of proposing a community-led alternative to demolition based on refurbishment and infill is the Carpenters Estate. Located in Newham, next to the Olympic Park, it is a very particular case. The local planning authority is the LLDC, while the land of the council estate is owned by Newham Council. Newham Council's intention is to demolish and redevelop the site with higher-density housing. The neighbourhood forum submitted their Neighbourhood Plan, which proposes 'refurbishment and sensitive infill', to the LLDC in June 2019. It has now gone through consultation and is with the independent examiner (see chapter 4).

Other neighbourhood areas are preparing Neighbourhood Plans that include council estates. However, Greater Carpenters Neighbourhood Forum is the only one whose main objective was to propose an alternative plan to council-led redevelopment.

Neighbourhood Development Order and Community Right to Build Order

Type of tool	Planning framework
National, GLA or Local level	National
Act, year	Localism Act 2011[25]
Regulations, year	The Neighbourhood Planning (General) Regulations 2012 (with updates and amendments)[26]
Guidance	Guidance Neighbourhood Planning[27]
See also:	Neighbourhood Planning: Neighbourhood Development Plan

Description of Neighbourhood Development Order and Community Right to Build Order

The Neighbourhood Development Order and the Community Right to Build Order are also part of the Localism Act 2011 and the Neighbourhood Planning Regulations. The Orders are designed to 'grant planning permission for specific types of development in a particular area'.[28]

A Neighbourhood Development Order can be used in combination with a Neighbourhood Plan (although doing a plan is not a prerequisite). When done in coordination with a Neighbourhood Plan, a Neighbourhood Development Order can grant planning permission to some of the uses proposed in the site allocations of the plan.[29]

The process for preparing a Neighbourhood Development Order has some similarities with a Neighbourhood Plan. Like a Neighbourhood Plan, it can be prepared by a parish or town council or a neighbourhood forum. Development Orders also must go through independent examination and be approved by referendum before they come into force.[30]

The Community Right to Build Order is a type of Neighbourhood Development Order that has strong potential for community-led social housing regeneration, since such Orders 'grant planning permission for small-scale, community-led developments'.[31] One of the advantages of a Community Right to Build Order is that the proposer, in addition to a parish or town council or neighbourhood forum, can also be a community organisation 'made up of individuals who live or work in the particular area for which the organisation is established'.[32] This makes it possible for local organisations to prepare a Community Right to Build Order for proposing their community-led development – which could be, for example, an infill housing development on a housing estate.

Usefulness for community-led social housing regeneration

Community Right to Build Orders can be particularly helpful for proposing infill developments that would provide new housing on the estate. It has recently been used by Leathermarket JMB to provide '27 new genuinely affordable homes on the former garage site'.[33]

Difficulties found and how to overcome them

One of the main difficulties for those using Community Right to Build Orders is that the organisation proposing it needs to have control over the land. In most housing estates, the land is owned by the council or a housing association. This means that the community can only execute this right if the land is available to them. This could depend on whether the landowner agrees to lease or sell them the land.

Difficulties can be also found in funding and delivering the development. In the section on technical and financial support, we provide some recommendations to help with these.

When we recommend to use this tool

The Community Right to Build Order can be used when the community has control over the land. The Locality guide advises that the Community Right to Build Order is a process that requires a lot of work, so it is only advisable when 'the land has been acquired or will be made available'.[34]

Technical and financial support available

The Mayor of London can use the 'London Community Housing Fund'[35] to fund community-led housing developments. The Mayor has also supported the creation of the Community-led Housing London Hub to provide 'funding and advice'[36] for community-led developments.

Cases of community-led social housing regeneration that have used this tool

The most significant case is Leathermarket JMB, an estate located in the London Borough of Southwark.[37] Leathermarket JMB is a 'resident-managed housing organisation', which manages '1500 homes in Borough and Bermondsey between London Bridge and Tower Bridge'.[38] They became a Tenant Management Organisation (TMO) in 1996 and gained the support of the residents, their mandate as managers being renewed in successive ballots. In April 2013 the organisation became a self-financing TMO, meaning that 'the organisation is able to retain all rent and service charges and thereby model a business plan over 30 years to deliver continuing improvements'.[39] In June 2015 they submitted the planning application to build '27 new, genuinely affordable homes on the former garage site'.[40] For the development, they created Leathermarket Community Benefit Society. The new infill homes, which have recently been completed, have won the 2019 New London Architecture Awards for Housing.[41]

Assets of Community Value and Community Right to Bid

Type of tool	Planning framework
National, GLA or Local level	National
Act, year	Localism Act 2011[42]
Regulations, year	The Assets of Community Value (England) Regulations 2012[43]
Guidance	Community Right to Bid: Non-statutory advice note for local authorities.[44] October 2012.
See also:	Neighbourhood Development Order; Community Right to Build Order

Description of Assets of Community Value and Community Right to Bid

A list of Assets of Community Value was introduced by the Localism Act 2011 (Part 5, Chapter 3). Community interest groups can nominate a building or land that has a social interest for the community – such as pubs, libraries, local shops, community centres or green spaces – to be registered in a list of Assets of Community Value. The aim of this regulation is to give community groups the opportunity of becoming potential bidders should the owner decide to sell the asset. This is intended to prevent the loss of places that are meaningful and relevant for local people, instead allowing the community to gain ownership and management of the place.

The process is quite simple since the group could be a neighbourhood forum or a group of 21 local people with no formal organisation; the nomination can be done in writing to the local authority. If nominated, the building or land remains on the list for five years. During this period, if the owner decides to sell it, they are obliged to inform the local authority. The community interest group will then have six weeks to show interest in bidding for the asset. If the community group do show interest, they will have six months from the time when the owner notified the local authority to raise funds to buy the asset. At the end of this period, the owner can sell it to the bidder they choose for the price they decide.[45, 46, 47]

Usefulness for community-led social housing regeneration

Communities can use this planning framework of the Localism Act to include parts of their estate in the listed Assets of Community Value, such as the community centre, any community facility, green space(s) or any place (publicly or privately owned) that is of significant value for the community. If the owner of the place, whether this is the council or a private individual, wants to sell it, the moratorium explained above will apply.

Difficulties found and how to overcome them

The process of including buildings and places in the listed Assets of Community Value does not itself have major difficulties. The major difficulty is actually to bid for buying the asset when/if at some point it is going to be sold. Being included in the list simply provides a moratorium, buying time for the community to raise funds. However, even if the community succeeds in raising funds to buy it, the asset's owner has the freedom of selling it to whoever they want. It is sold on the open market and they have no obligation or commitment to sell it to the community.

For overcoming this difficulty, it is important to get financial advice. Locality provide support on the Community Right to Bid and have produced a guide for this,[48] and government funding, is available through the programme for 'Community Ownership and Management of Assets'.[49]

When we recommend to use this tool

Residents living in social housing estates can use this tool to include their community facilities, community infrastructure and other eligible buildings of community interest in the list. In case the owner wants to sell the asset, there will be a moratorium, which can allow the community some time to raise funds.

Technical and financial support available

Locality offers support for communities who want to bid for a community asset. Communities can contact Locality through the email that appears on their website for Assets of Community Value.[50] In their guide, they also mention the government's grant programme for 'Community Ownership and Management of Assets'.[51]

Cases of community-led social housing regeneration that have used this tool

Greater Carpenters Neighbourhood Forum and Cressingham Gardens residents have been successful in including their community buildings in the listed Assets of Community Value. So far, neither of these two groups has bid for these assets, as they have not yet been put on the market.

Notes

1. See Claire Colomb. 2017. 'Participation and Conflict in the Formation of Neighbourhood Areas and Forums in "Super-Diverse" Cities', in Sue Brownill and Quintin Bradley, eds., *Localism and Neighbourhood Planning*. Policy Press: Bristol; and Elena Besussi. 2018. 'Localism and Neighbourhood Planning', in J. Ferm and J. Tomaney, eds., *Planning Practice. Critical Perspectives from the UK*. Routledge: London.
2. Localism Act 2011. http://www.legislation.gov.uk/ukpga/2011/20/contents/enacted. Accessed 1 August 2019.

3. The Neighbourhood Planning (General) Regulations 2012. http://www.legislation.gov.uk/uksi/2012/637/contents/made. Accessed 1 August 2019.

4. Ministry of Housing, Communities and Local Government. 2014; 2019. 'Guidance: Neighbourhood Planning'. Published 6 March 2014; last updated 9 May 2019. https://www.gov.uk/guidance/neighbourhood-planning–2. Accessed 1 August 2019.

5. Locality. 2016. 'Neighbourhood Plans Roadmap Guide'. An updated version of this guide can be found on https://neighbourhoodplanning.org/wp-content/uploads/NP_Roadmap_online_full.pdf. Accessed 31 July 2019.

6. The information here is extracted from Locality. 2016. 'Neighbourhood Plans Road Map Guide'. The Neighbourhood Planning (General) Regulations 2012 and 'Guidance: Neighbourhood Planning'.

7. Locality. 2016. 'Neighbourhood Plans Road Map Guide'.

8. Department for Communities and Local Government. 2014. 'Community Infrastructure Levy'. https://www.gov.uk/guidance/community-infrastructure-levy. Accessed 31 May 2017.

9. Cecil Sagoe. 2016. 'One Tool Amongst Many: Considering the Political Potential of Neighbourhood Planning for the Greater Carpenters Neighbourhood, London', *Architecture, Media, Politics and Society* 9(3): 1–20.

10. NeighbourhoodPlanners.London. 2017. 'London's Local Plans: Are They Supporting Neighbourhood Planning?', 3. http://docs.wixstatic.com/ugd/95f6a3_6d2d4b5b624c44fd963fedcea470d28d.pdf. Accessed 31 July 2019.

11. NeighbourhoodPlanners.London. 2017. 'London's Local Plans: Are They Supporting Neighbourhood Planning?', 2.

12. NeighbourhoodPlanners.London. 2017. 'London's Local Plans: Are They Supporting Neighbourhood Planning?', 1.

13. Gavin Parker, Tessa Lynn and Matthew Wargent. 2014. 'User Experience of Neighbourhood Planning in England. London'. Report. Locality. 2014. http://mycommunity.org.uk/wp-content/uploads/2016/08/User-experience-executive-study.pdf. Accessed 31 May 2017. Referenced in Civil Exchange. 2015. *Whose Society? The Final Big Society Audit.* http://www.civilexchange.org.uk/wp-content/uploads/2015/01/Whose-Society_The-Final-Big-Society-Audit_final.pdf. Accessed 3 March 2017.

14. Interview with Richard Lee, Just Space coordinator, 18 January 2017.

15. Department for Communities and Local Government. 2014. 'Community Infrastructure Levy'.

16. Department for Communities and Local Government. 2014. 'Community Infrastructure Levy'.

17. For more information on issues related to Community Infrastructure Levy, see Neighbourhood Planners. London's report on Community Infrastructure Levy: Neighbourhood Planners.London. 2016. Neighbourhood Element of the Community Infrastructure Levy (CIL): The London Experience. https://www.neighbourhoodplanners.london/resources. Accessed 23 January 2020.

18. Sagoe. 2016. 'One Tool Amongst Many: Considering the Political Potential of Neighbourhood Planning for the Greater Carpenters Neighbourhood, London'.

19. Sagoe. 2016. 'One Tool Amongst Many: Considering the Political Potential of Neighbourhood Planning for the Greater Carpenters Neighbourhood, London'.

20. Locality. 'About'. https://neighbourhoodplanning.org. Accessed 31 July 2019.

21. Locality. 'About'. http://locality.org.uk/about/. Accessed 21 February 2017.

22. Locality. 'About'. http://locality.org.uk/about/. Accessed 21 February 2017.

23. My Community, Locality. https://mycommunity.org.uk. Accessed 31 July 2019.

24. Neighbourhood Planning, Locality. https://neighbourhoodplanning.org. Accessed 26 November 2019.

25. Localism Act 2011.

26. The Neighbourhood Planning (General) Regulations 2012.

27. Ministry of Housing, Communities and Local Government. 'Guidance: Neighbourhood Planning'.

28. Neighbourhood Planning, Locality. 2018. 'Neighbourhood Development Orders (Including Community Right to Build Orders)'. https://neighbourhoodplanning.org/toolkits-and-guidance/neighbourhood-development-orders-community-right-build-orders/. Accessed 1 August 2019.

29. Neighbourhood Planning, Locality. 'Neighbourhood Development Orders (including Community Right to Build Orders)'. https://neighbourhoodplanning.org/toolkits-and-guidance/neighbourhood-development-orders-community-right-build-orders/. Accessed 1 August 2019.

30. Neighbourhood Planning, Locality. 'Neighbourhood Development Orders (Including Community Right to Build Orders)'. https://neighbourhoodplanning.org/toolkits-and-guidance/neighbourhood-development-orders-community-right-build-orders/. Accessed 1 August 2019.
31. Neighbourhood Planning, Locality. 'Neighbourhood Development Orders (Including Community Right to Build Orders)', 4. https://neighbourhoodplanning.org/toolkits-and-guidance/neighbourhood-development-orders-community-right-build-orders/. Accessed 1 August 2019.
32. Neighbourhood Planning, Locality. 'Neighbourhood Development Orders (Including Community Right to Build Orders)', 8. https://neighbourhoodplanning.org/toolkits-and-guidance/neighbourhood-development-orders-community-right-build-orders/. Accessed 1 August 2019.
33. Leathermarket JMB. 'Who are Leathermarket JMB?'. http://www.leathermarketjmb.org.uk/about-jmb/. Accessed 1 August 2019.
34. Neighbourhood Planning, Locality. 'Neighbourhood Development Orders (Including Community Right to Build Orders)', 15. https://neighbourhoodplanning.org/toolkits-and-guidance/neighbourhood-development-orders-community-right-build-orders/. Accessed 1 August 2019.
35. Mayor of London. January 2019. 'London Community Housing Fund'. https://www.london.gov.uk/sites/default/files/london_chf_prospectus_0.pdf. Accessed 1 August 2019.
36. Community-led Housing London. https://www.communityledhousing.london. Accessed 1 August 2019.
37. This case study was pointed out to me (Pablo Sendra) by Cecilia Colombo and Alice Devenyns, students from the Civic Design CPD course. It is included in the report resulting from the course: Aggie Morris, Alice Devenyns, Cecilia Colombo, Dolors Vila, Dominic Cort, Iacovos Loizou, Irene Manzini Ceinar, Leslie Barson, Ursula Wyss, Pablo Sendra. 2019. *Towards a Co-Design Process: An Alternative to Demolition for William Dunbar and William Saville Tower Blocks, South Kilburn*. London: Civic Design CPD Course. The Bartlett School of Planning, UCL.
38. Leathermarket JMB. 'Who are Leathermarket JMB?'. http://www.leathermarketjmb.org.uk/about-jmb/. Accessed 1 August 2019.
39. Leathermarket JMB. 'Who are Leathermarket JMB?'. http://www.leathermarketjmb.org.uk/about-jmb/. Accessed 1 August 2019.
40. Leathermarket JMB. 'Who are Leathermarket JMB?'. http://www.leathermarketjmb.org.uk/about-jmb/. Accessed 1 August 2019.
41. New London Architecture. 2019. 'New London Awards 2019 Winners'. https://www.newlondonarchitecture.org/whats-on/new-london-awards/new-london-awards/new-london-awards-2019-winners. Accessed 1 August 2019.
42. Localism Act 2011.
43. The Assets of Community Value (England) Regulations 2012. http://www.legislation.gov.uk/uksi/2012/2421/contents/made. Accessed 1 August 2019.
44. Department for Communities and Local Government. October 2012. 'Community Right to Bid: Non-Statutory Advice Note for Local Authorities'. https://assets.publishing.service.gov.uk/government/uploads/system/uploads/attachment_data/file/14880/Community_Right_to_Bid_-_Non-statutory_advice_note_for_local_authorities.pdf. Accessed 1 August 2019.
45. My Community, Locality. 'Assets of Community Value & Right to Bid'. https://mycommunity.org.uk/take-action/land-and-building-assets/assets-of-community-value-right-to-bid/. Accessed 31 July 2019.
46. Localism Act 2011.
47. The Assets of Community Value (England) Regulations 2012.
48. My Community, Locality; The Social Investment Business; Local Government Regulation. 2016. 'Community Right to Bid: Understanding the Community Right to Bid'. https://mycommunity.org.uk/wp-content/uploads/2016/09/Understanding-the-Community-Right-to-Bid.pdf. Accessed 1 August 2019.
49. My Community, Locality; The Social Investment Business; Local Government Regulation. 'Community Right to Bid: Understanding the Community Right to Bid'. https://mycommunity.org.uk/wp-content/uploads/2016/09/Understanding-the-Community-Right-to-Bid.pdf. Accessed 1 August 2019.
50. My Community, Locality; The Social Investment Business; Local Government Regulation. 'Community Right to Bid: Understanding the Community Right to Bid'. https://mycommunity.org.uk/wp-content/uploads/2016/09/Understanding-the-Community-Right-to-Bid.pdf. Accessed 1 August 2019.
51. My Community, Locality; The Social Investment Business; Local Government Regulation. 'Community Right to Bid: Understanding the Community Right to Bid'. https://mycommunity.org.uk/wp-content/uploads/2016/09/Understanding-the-Community-Right-to-Bid.pdf. Accessed 1 August 2019.

10
Policies for community participation in regeneration

There are formal policy tools for community participation in regeneration, from national to local level. Activists as well as academics have been debating and contesting them, but nonetheless they are shaping how residents are involved in regeneration. Looking back, the debate around community participation in the UK first emerged in the 1960s. A Planning Advisory Group report on The Future of Development Plans in 1965 led to the set-up of the Skeffington Committee to look at the participation of the public in local development plans.[1] Published in 1969, the Skeffington Report stated that plans should be subject to full public scrutiny and debate.[2] This was, however, quite a limited way of considering participation in the planning process, especially when regeneration was considered.

The scope of community participation has evolved and now, although there have been attempts to standardise the requirement to involve communities, it often depends on how different communities view proposals and the scale of the policies to be implemented. What remains critical is the nature of the participation , the notion of community that is used and the power relations that exist during implementation of policy into plans. The following examples are policy tools which affect regeneration at different scales – from the government's national strategy on regeneration down to city-scale policies, such as the London Plan and the London Housing Strategy, and so to the smaller scale policies of an estate, where ballots may be key to the decision-making process involved in regeneration.

The London Plan and the London Housing Strategy are both examples of city-scale policies that include community participation. Although there are no city-regions or unitary authorities with the governance or scale of London, there are currently statutory joint strategic plans, spatial development strategies, joint local plans, aligned strategies and non-statutory strategic planning frameworks being carried out across England, across unitary councils, county councils and metropolitan city-regions. Among these are the Liverpool City Region Spatial Development Strategy, the Greater Manchester Spatial Framework and the Newcastle Gateshead Joint Core Strategy. All of these are emerging documents, although the extent or coordination of community involvement remains to be seen. London is therefore a precursor in many ways and, as pointed out in the 'Introduction', it offers some important lessons on the role of community involvement in shaping planning policy at the metropolitan level – both through the formal routes of consultation and the informal routes of developing strong and effective counter-proposals through community-led campaigns.

This section explores the tools which are not necessarily for residents to use, but which are shaping policy on regeneration for local authorities and housing associations. It is useful for residents and community groups to know about these, however, so that they can put into context the regeneration agendas that are being promoted and which they are affected by, and which they are developing campaigns to oppose. They can, as policies, also be used to challenge current bad practice, which may not conform to national or London-wide policy.

Some of the only direct housing regeneration which is properly community-led is being supported by the Community-led Housing Hub. This is designed for residents, but has not really yet addressed the case for estate regeneration.

The policies below therefore sit in a context of shifting regeneration, housing and broader planning agendas which are particular to urban areas in the UK. The focus of the case studies has been London, and therefore the policies below are seen from the capital's perspective. But, as explored in the 'Introduction', the importance for residents lies not necessarily in the specific policies but rather in how coordination between different tools, strategies and policies has drawn together groups in the movement, enabling them to move from opposition to proposition for their own community-led forms of regeneration. This points to linkages that can be made to housing and regeneration struggles and proposals emerging in other cities – not only in the UK, but also in Europe and beyond. Here the important thing is to understand the linkages and coordination between tools, strategies and actors.

Government's Estate Regeneration National Strategy

Type of tool	Strategy
National, GLA or Local level	National
Regulations, year	Estate Regeneration National Strategy (December 2016)

Description of the government's Estate Regeneration National Strategy

The government's strategy on estate regeneration was published in December 2016. It outlines its aspiration for the transformation of neighbourhoods through the delivery of high-quality, well-designed housing and public spaces. The strategy offers a range of practical guidance to support recognised local partners, including residents, to improve the quality and delivery of estate regeneration schemes. The opening section features guidance for landlords, developers and local authorities on how to engage residents throughout the estate regeneration process. In particular, the role of local authorities is recognised, as is how they can take a lead in the process. Guidance is given also on financing and the delivery of estate regeneration schemes, through partnerships and the leverage of private investment.

Essentially a good practice guide, the strategy establishes the key considerations for projects and offers a model process for successful regeneration in the form of an activity map. This sets out the path of a model estate regeneration scheme, and also includes a design and quality checklist related to the design of schemes. The strategy aims to improve social outcomes and proposes piloting of spend-mapping analysis. It focuses on key public services such as crime and policing, health and welfare benefits to help coordinate funding. A section includes community-led housing as an alternative, defined here as homes that are developed or managed by local people or residents. The strategy then outlines co-operative housing, Community Land Trusts, development trusts, self-help and self-build housing, community-led housing associations, mutuals and almshouses. Partner organisations are reviewed and case studies offered as good practice in estate regeneration.

Usefulness for community-led social housing regeneration

The strategy offers a guide to good practice supported by models, which can be used to call out councils or developers that are not undertaking regeneration as recommended. It also provides guidance for community participation, engagement and protection. The national strategy is accompanied by some funding, including £140 million (loans for private sector and private registered providers), £30 million (enabling grants for local authorities or registered providers) and £2 million (capacity-building funding for local authorities), which would be made available to support estate regeneration. Such funding is also seen as a way to lessen risk in the early stages of projects, as well as to provide support for more community involvement.

Difficulties in the case of community-led social housing regeneration

There is much in the strategy that could be commended at an advisory level. However, the main opportunity offered for community-led housing regeneration lies in the section on alternative approaches. Many of the case studies presented appear to be more problematic, involving the demolition of social housing stock and replacement with higher-income tenures, displacement and social cleansing, overall privatisation of public land and management. The issues of changes to social tenures and overall management, including the viability processes of regeneration schemes, remain unaddressed in the strategy. As a result, many of the main issues that communities face as part of regeneration are not discussed in this document. However, the government's strategy on estate regeneration does offer a level of 'good practice' and standards, which can be used to refer to in cases where even these standards are not being met.

London Plan

Type of tool	Planning document
National, GLA or Local level	Greater London Authority
Regulations, year	London Plan (draft new Plan consolidated version July 2019)
See also:	London Housing Strategy

Description of the London Plan

The London Plan is a strategic document that lays out policy on how London should develop over the next 20–25 years.[3] It covers housing, design, social infrastructure, the economy, heritage and culture, green space and the natural environment, sustainable infrastructure, including air quality, emissions and waste, and transport, as well as some specific strategies and places (Opportunity Areas) for growth. Legally, the London Plan sits as part of the 32 London boroughs' development plans and must be taken into account in their decision-making.

The first plan was produced in 2004 and the current plan in 2016. A draft new London Plan is now also available. It broadly covers the strategy for London with an economic, environmental, transport and social framework for the capital's future. The new Plan brings together geographic and locational aspects of strategies dealing with transport, economic development, housing and culture, as well as social issues such as children, health inequalities and food. It also has measures to tackle

Figure 10.1 Just Space and other community organisations participating in the Examination in Public of the London Plan, February 2019. Image: Pablo Sendra.

a range of environmental issues such as climate change (adaptation and mitigation), air quality, noise and waste.

The new Plan is currently under review by the Mayor of London after having gone through consultation and the Examination in Public process (fig.10.1) and after having received the Inspector's Report on 8 October 2019.[4] The latest draft version of the Plan with consolidated changes was released after the Examination in Public in July 2019.[5] The Plan opens with six Good Growth policies, which include building strong and inclusive communities, making the best use of land, creating a healthy city, delivering the homes that Londoners need, growing a good economy and increasing efficiency and resilience. The other policies then sit alongside these Good Growth policies.

Usefulness for community-led social housing regeneration

One of the most useful things to note about the actual Plan has been the process through which the draft Plan has been scrutinised and examined. The chapters have all been available for consultation and submissions; responses have now been collected and groups have been invited to the six-month process of Examination in Public led by a Planning Inspector. This has meant thousands of submissions, including those from a range of community groups, such as the ones coordinated by Just Space. The main thrust of Just Space's responses followed the lines that they developed in their alternative London Plan, Towards a Community-Led London Plan.[6] This included a range of particular policies with regard to community-led social housing support, some of which have been included in the new draft Plan.

Where next with the London Plan

Following the Examination in Public, the draft London Plan was consolidated into a version that showed the suggested changes of the Mayor in July 2019. The Panel submitted the Inspector's Report to the Mayor in October 2019. The latest update from the Mayor of London and the London Assembly's website is:

> The Mayor is currently considering the Panel report and recommendations and is preparing an Intend to Publish version of the London Plan which will be sent to the Secretary of State, alongside a schedule of the panel's recommendation and the Mayor's response to

them. It is envisaged the Intend to Publish version of the Plan will be sent to the Secretary of State and published online by the end of the year.[7]

A number of wider issues in the draft London Plan remain problematic and need to be addressed. They are likely to affect any form of community-led planning, including regeneration, and were clearly evident during the Examination in Public. The first is the serious endeavour on the part of community groups to articulate and apply throughout the Plan the legislation of the Equality Act 2010 and the obligation of the GLA under the Public Sector Equality Duty (see chapter 11 on challenging regeneration through the legal system).

Issues of equality have therefore been taken seriously for the first time by the inspectors involved,[8] who insisted that the Mayor report urgently on the expected impacts of the Plan on each of the groups in society protected by law. This in part was a response to the challenge made by Just Space,[9] which claimed that the housing proposals would fail to satisfy the GLA's obligations under the Public Sector Equality Duty.

As Just Space point out, the response by the GLA to this request was 'a fascinating essay on the diversity of needs among Londoners'. If used earlier in the process, the analysis based on the nine equality groups (age, disability, gender reassignment, marriage and civil partnership, pregnancy and maternity, race, religion or belief, sex, sexual orientation) would have enriched the drafting of the London Plan. They also point out that the social class dimension is not dealt with explicitly, but note that there are strong overlaps between poverty and group experiences of deprivation.[10]

The second main critical point is that the Plan has weak 'affordable' housing proposals, which fail to meet the needs identified by the Mayor for low-rent council housing. Instead there continues to be an explicit support for the types of housing, indeed the sort of growth, that relatively few Londoners can afford.[11] This has been reiterated by a wide range of organisations, ranging from Just Space, the London Tenants Federation and the 35% Campaign, to the Council for the Preservation of Rural England and the Highbury Group, who had made independent critiques. Even the way in which the term 'affordable' has now transformed into 'genuinely affordable', and is accompanied by a range of definitions for different rental levels, continues to complicate and obfuscate the underlying need and imperative to build social housing at rents which people in London can pay.

This issue is then connected to the related concerns around the importance still placed on the use of viability appraisals at the heart of any regeneration or development proposal. Lesser consideration is given towards the broader forms of value created, the impacts on existing and future communities, and seriously tackling the need for social housing, let alone community-led social housing.

London Housing Strategy

Type of tool	Strategy
National, GLA or Local level	Greater London Authority
Regulations, year	London Housing Strategy
See also:	London Plan
	Mayor's Good Practice Guide to Estate
	Regeneration

Description of the London Housing Strategy

The London Housing Strategy defines the Mayor's vision on housing in London and was approved in August 2018.[12] 'Tackling the London housing crisis', as the Mayor frames it, provides a strategy for the different actors involved in the delivery of housing and a series of policies to achieve its objectives. The five priorities of the strategy are building homes for Londoners, the delivery of genuinely affordable homes, the development of high-quality homes and inclusive neighbourhoods, putting into place a fairer deal for private renters and leaseholders, and tackling homelessness and helping rough sleepers.

Particularly relevant for estate regeneration are the chapters on tackling issues of affordability and the involvement of the community in the delivery of homes. This includes policies to increase the numbers of affordable homes, of which some are social rented homes defined as London Affordable Homes, at London Living Rent, and Shared Ownership. Protection is also given to existing affordable homes, as they cannot be converted to higher rental category homes. Those homes that are sold under Right to Buy or demolished through regeneration need to be replaced locally on a like-for-like basis.

Usefulness for community-led social housing regeneration

The overall aim is to increase delivery of social housing. There are policies designed to protect the existing social housing, with like-for-like replacement of social housing when homes are demolished through redevelopment or sold through the Right to Buy. This can prevent bad practices of estate redevelopment resulting in massive loss of social housing, such as the case of the Heygate Estate in the London Borough of Southwark. The document also establishes a threshold proportion of affordable housing 'by providing a Fast Track Route through the planning system for developers that provide at least 35 per cent affordable homes without public subsidy, or 50 per cent on public land or industrial sites'.[13]

The strategy does offer support for community groups to deliver housing, as it has within it two specific actions on community-led developments. These include the launch of the Community-led Housing Hub for London and the offer of investment, including a share of the national community housing fund. Technical and funding support, through the hub, is offered when schemes provide genuinely affordable housing.

Difficulties found in the use of community-led social housing regeneration

Although the strategy refers to the involvement of residents in decisions and the need to hear their voices, it is not specific on the mechanisms and requirements to achieve this. Also, in terms of consultation, hearing is not necessarily listening to achieve this, still less acting upon. The strategy does cross-reference the Mayor's Good Practice Guide to Estate Regeneration, which has a dedicated chapter on the involvement of residents in regeneration. However, the strategy does not mention any other neighbourhood planning tools that could potentially offer ways in which communities could make decisions about future developments in their areas, other than the Resident Ballot for estate redevelopment schemes. This is especially true of the neighbourhood planning tools available in the Localism Act 2011 (see chapter 9).

The Housing Strategy's proposal for the Community-led Housing Hub, which has already been established, could potentially be a resource for community-led developments. However, the role of the Community-led Housing Hub is currently directed at developments on small sites; it does not explicitly apply to community-led social housing regeneration. The hub could support residents who would like to develop their own strategies or even plans on existing social housing estates that may require refurbishment, retrofitting and infill strategies. This issue was discussed in the Just Space conference organised to produce a collective response to the consultation on the Draft London Housing Strategy (fig.10.2).

Recent years have seen huge progress in gaining policy and funding support from the GLA and government for community-led housing generally. When communities are bringing forward proposals that are in line with government, GLA or council ambitions, the propositions and initiatives are being funded and supported at the level needed.

However, many of the case studies we have looked at in the first part of the book are pursuing projects that are generally either in opposition to their council, or at least challenge the council's proposals for regeneration and try to propose another direction for regeneration – in effect moving from the oppositional to the propositional. The GLA has tended not to take a view on these proposals, except broadly to support the councils involved. More broadly, the community-led housing sector has had to tread a delicate path – not only to negotiate and develop an

Figure 10.2 Workshop on 'Community-Led Estate Regeneration' during Just Space conference on the consultation on the Draft London Housing Strategy, November 2017. Image: Pablo Sendra.

increasingly supportive relationship with government, but also, at the same time, look at how they can support community groups and campaigns exploring the possibility of taking the lead in the regeneration of their estate. Such campaigns are trying to utilise the community-led housing agenda as part of the wider policies on regeneration led more by community groups.

'Better Homes for Local People' – The Mayor's Good Practice Guide to Estate Regeneration

Type of tool	Good practice guide
National, GLA or Local level	Greater London Authority
Regulations, year	*Better Homes for Local People* – The Mayor's Good Practice Guide to Estate Regeneration
See also:	Resident ballot requirement The Mayor's draft Good Practice Guide to Estate Regeneration – Consultation Summary Report Government's Estate Regeneration National Strategy – Resident Engagement and Protection Guide

Description of the Mayor's Good Practice Guide to Estate Regeneration

The draft Good Practice Guide was published in December 2016.[14] With the aim of laying out some of the good practices for future London estate regeneration, the Mayor of London stated in the foreword that he wanted 'to see existing local residents closely involved from the outset'.[15] The report had three sections focusing on the aims and objectives of estate regeneration. These included maintenance, supply of new housing and improving the social, economic and physical environments, the consultation and engagement with residents and achieving a fair deal for both tenants and leaseholders. A range of case studies of estate regenerations were outlined, but no distinction was made between those projects that had already been completed and those that were ongoing. Each chapter ended with a range of good practice proposals.

The consultation ran from December 2016 through to March 2017, and a range of responses were reflected upon and shaped some of the changes.[16] These came from a variety of civil society and housing campaign groups from across London, including Architects for Social Housing

(ASH), 35% campaign, Barnet Housing Action Group, Demolition Watch, Just Space, Northwold Estate campaign group and the London Tenants Federation (LTF). Among the submissions was also a collective response from a cross-section of academics, policy-makers, regeneration specialists, housing activists, community groups, council tenants and leaseholders, social housing providers and other organisations that have either worked with council tenants and leaseholders or conducted research on social housing across London, or that have experienced first-hand the effects of estate regeneration, coordinated by Professor Loretta Lees.[17]

The three chapters of the guide included good practices drawn from case studies of past and current housing regeneration schemes. The responses to the draft noted that the aims and objectives of estate regeneration should be set out clearly with residents, who should then have the chance to shape these proposals and have their comments incorporated in a meaningful way. Consideration should be given not only to the options available, but also to how combinations of physical interventions could work for residents, including refurbishment, infill, demolition and rebuild.[18] The latter options should only take place when the process does not result in a net loss of social housing and other options have been exhausted. The appearance and relationship of the estate with the surrounding area should be improved, and the impacts and outcomes of the work should be monitored.

Chapter 2 of the guide went into more detail over consultation and monitoring procedures, including tenant involvement and the funding of independent advisers. The final chapter outlined how a fair deal for both tenants and leaseholders must be ensured, including addressing the issues of rehousing, compensation and advice. This included increasing affordable housing, giving full rights to return or remain for social tenants, and providing a fair deal for leaseholders and freeholders. The case studies also looked at the management of the 'moving process' or displacement of original residents. The guide outlined the need to have full compensation for inconvenience and to ensure high priority for rehousing. Where possible social tenants should only move once, and they should be 'offered full rights to return to suitable homes with same or similar rents'. Leaseholders should be offered payments which are at market value plus home-loss payments. According to the guide, they should also be offered shared equity or shared ownership in the new housing.

Finally, the guidance also included examples of some charters which local authorities or housing associations have used to make explicit their relationship with residents. These could also be formulated or co-produced in the future by both residents and developing agents. In any case, the guidance should be read alongside statutory housing and planning policy documents. The intention is that the guide will be put into practice as part of the Mayor's funding conditions, and future estate regeneration funded by the Mayor will have to conform to these principles. However, even in situations where the Mayor is not involved, the guide can inform proposals for estate renewal.

Difficulties found and how to overcome them

The main problems raised by groups in response to the draft, not all of which were addressed in the final version of the guidance, were related mainly to the engagement of residents and leaseholders in the process of estate regeneration. In particular, this concerned the implementation of a series of proposals including the introduction of some form of independent ballot (which was introduced after the consultation, but as a condition of GLA funding), consideration of all tenures, the legal precedents for proper consultation, the right of return and the funding of independent advisers. One particular aspect, which remained overlooked, was the wider issue of how to capture the value uplift for community benefit and the problematics of proper, longer-term monitoring of impacts. The continued use of the word 'affordable' remains problematic, as there is a constant slippage between social rent and affordable rent. Other phrases remain devoid of concrete meaning based on a shared understanding, among them 'bottom-up process', 'right to return', 'robust' or 'transparent' consultations.

There thus needs to be more than just verbal commitment to 'bottom-up' resident involvement, as financial commitments are also required to facilitate that involvement. Not only does consultation need to be transparent, extensive, responsive and meaningful, as the GLA document states,[19] but all viable options must also be considered as early as possible. Considerations of costs and benefits in financial, social and environmental terms must be allowed, and these costs should not focus solely on the opaque viability assessments, which have been used to justify reducing the numbers of social housing across developments.[20] Consultation should be conducted primarily with social tenants and leaseholders, but the views of other affected people must also be included, using a range of engagement methods enabling greater and sustained participation.

Overall there is a strong need to protect the dwindling stock of social rented homes, as there has been a serious decrease in the numbers available (–8000 since 2005) in London. Therefore, monitoring and oversight should be longitudinal, funded independently, made up of experts and community groups and, critically, enforceable. The consultation and engagement section needs a 'more thoroughgoing recognition of the rights of residents'.[21] Ballots should be pivotal and mandatory, and 'residents need to be able to vote on a range of proposals, including ones they have been involved in drawing-up'.[22] The security of tenures, including leaseholders, should be ensured and guarantees put in place around respecting same rent levels if individuals are displaced or moved. This should include the right to stay put, over and above the right to return. The guidance should specify that 'estate redevelopment ensures a net increase in council housing (the only truly affordable housing for low-income Londoners) given London's housing crisis'.[23]

Resident ballots for estate regeneration project

Type of tool	Funding condition for regeneration
National, GLA or Local level	Greater London Authority
Regulations, year	Affordable Housing Capital Funding Guide, Section 8[24]
See also:	Mayor's Good Practice Guide to Estate Regeneration

Context

As a result of the public consultation on the Mayor of London's Good Practice Guide to Estate Regeneration (discussed above) that took place between December 2016 and March 2017, a lot of responses requested a Resident ballot, in which the residents would be able to vote on whether they wanted the redevelopment of their estate or not. This request for a ballot appeared in Just Space's response to the consultation,[25] as well as in a petition by Demolition Watch.[26] The Mayor of London then consulted on the Resident ballot regulation between February and April 2018, and brought it into force in July 2018.

However, the Mayor did not make the Resident ballot a requirement for getting planning approval of the redevelopment of an estate; it is rather a condition of obtaining GLA funding for affordable housing. This fact was not welcomed by community groups. The fact that a Freedom of Information (FOI) request showed that a number of estate redevelopments that imply demolition had received funding from the GLA just two months before the consultation process was also quite controversial.[27] The Resident ballot funding condition came into force in July 2018, as noted above. Since then, a few estates have gone through the process.

A tool for councils, housing associations and/or developers, not for residents

A Resident ballot is a tool for the 'Investment Partners'[28] of the estate. They are the ones who make the decisions on when the ballot is held, what the questions on the ballot should be, the nature of the redevelopment proposal itself and the information that residents receive. Residents themselves have no control of the process (the regeneration or redevelopment proposal, the offer for those needing to be rehoused, the question(s) being asked on the ballot), apart from voting in the ballot. There is no requirement for the Investment Partners to co-produce either the redevelopment proposals or the ballot process with the residents. The ballot is thus a consultation controlled by the Investment Partners (although they must hire an independent body to run the actual voting process), not a participation process. The only situation in which residents can control the ballot is when the Investment Partners are a resident-managed organisation.

When a ballot applies and who is eligible to vote

The ballot applies when any home (affordable or leasehold, see details on tenure in the regulation)[29] is going to be demolished on a housing estate and more than 150 new homes are going to be built within the boundaries of the existing estate.[30]

The boundaries of an existing housing estate, as the regulation recognises, can be interpreted in different ways. This is quite relevant, since the definition of the boundary of the estate can have an impact on the ballot's outcome. According to the voter eligibility requirements, '(b)allots must be open to all residents on an existing social housing estate – not just those currently occupying homes that are due to be demolished'.[31] Defining the boundary of an estate can thus have an impact on the outcome of the ballot.

The eligibility criteria also establish that those with the right to vote are social tenants (which includes intermediate affordable housing), leaseholders or freeholders when their property is their principal home, as well as '(a)ny resident whose principal home is on the estate who has been on the local authority's housing register for at least one year'.[32]

Advantages of the ballot

The Resident ballot funding condition, although insufficient, supposes progress in the rights of residents during a redevelopment process. Local authorities rely on funding from the GLA for delivering affordable housing, and this ballot funding condition sets up certain requirements that did not exist before. The regulation has been in place only for a year. Community organisations and scholars supporting them should look at the ballots that are taking place in order to require fairer ballots in which residents have stronger decision-making powers. This means not just voting, but also having decision-making power to co-produce the proposals, determine the question(s) and contribute to the information supplied for the ballot.

Things to consider carefully

When residents are subject to a ballot on their estate, they should ensure that the ballot is run in compliance with the GLA regulations.[33] Things that residents should look at particularly are:

- Voter eligibility requirement: make sure the voter eligibility criteria that the Investment Partners are proposing meet the requirements established by the Mayor of London. Note that residents living in temporary accommodation and other residents on the estate who are not social tenants, leaseholders or freeholders can only vote if they have been on the local authority's housing register for at least one year.
- Look carefully at the how the boundary of the estate is defined. The regulations say the ballot should be carried out by the Investment Partners. That means that all the redevelopment should have the same Investment Partners. The regulation itself recognises that the definition of the boundaries is ambiguous, and recommends Investment Partners to seek advice from the GLA when this is not clear. The boundary of the estate can have influence on the outcome of the ballot, as it defines who can and who cannot vote. For this reason, it is important for residents to scrutinise this and to contact the GLA if they feel the boundary is not correctly drawn.

- Residents must require that they are given sufficient information to make an informed decision. See chapter 11 on what legally constitutes a fair consultation.

Notes

1. Planning Advisory Group. 1965. *The Future of Development Plans*. HMSO: London.
2. Arthur Skeffington. 1969. *People and Planning. Report of the Committee on Public Participation in Planning*. HMSO: London.
3. The draft new London Plan was published in 2018 and has been going through a process of Examination in Public (EiP). The consolidated version was published in July 2019: 'Draft London Plan'. https://www.london.gov.uk/what-we-do/planning/london-plan/new-london-plan/draft-london-plan-consolidated-suggested-changes-version-july-2019. Accessed 1 August 2019.
4. Mayor of London, London Assembly. 2019. 'Inspector's Report'. https://www.london.gov.uk/what-we-do/planning/london-plan/new-london-plan/inspectors-report. Accessed 29 November 2019.
5. Mayor of London, London Assembly. 2019. 'Draft London Plan – Consolidated Suggested Changes Version July 2019'. https://www.london.gov.uk/what-we-do/planning/london-plan/new-london-plan/draft-london-plan-consolidated-suggested-changes-version-july-2019. Accessed 1 August 2019.
6. Just Space. 2016. 'Towards a Community-Led Plan for London: Policy Directions and Proposals'. https://justspace.org.uk/the-community-led-alternative-plan. Accessed 1 August 2019.
7. Mayor of London, London Assembly. 2019. 'Inspector's Report'.
8. Just Space. 2019. 'Inspectors Taking Equality Seriously'. https://justspace.org.uk/2019/03/13/inspectors-taking-equality-seriously. Accessed 1 August 2019.
9. Just Space. 2019. 'Grave Weaknesses in the London Plan'. https://justspace.org.uk/2019/02/26/grave-weaknesses-in-the-london-plan. Accessed 1 August 2019.
10. Just Space. 2019. 'Actual Equalities Study at Last'. https://justspace.org.uk/2019/04/28/actual-equalities-study-at-last. Accessed 1 August 2019.
11. Just Space. 2019. 'Grave Weaknesses in the London Plan'. https://justspace.org.uk/2019/02/26/grave-weaknesses-in-the-london-plan. Accessed 1 August 2019.
12. Mayor of London, London Assembly. 2018. 'Tackling London's Housing Crisis'. https://www.london.gov.uk/what-we-do/housing-and-land/tackling-londons-housing-crisis. Accessed 1 August 2019.
13. Mayor of London. 2018. *London Housing Strategy*. London: Greater London Authority. https://www.london.gov.uk/sites/default/files/2018_lhs_london_housing_strategy.pdf. Accessed 29 November 2019.
14. These comments refer to the first draft that was published in 2016 as the *Good Practice Guide to Estate Regeneration*. The Mayor addressed some of the issues raised, published as *Better Homes for Local People: The Mayor's Good Practice Guide to Estate Regeneration*. https://www.london.gov.uk/what-we-do/housing-and-land/improving-quality/estate-regeneration. Accessed 23 January 2020.
15. Mayor of London, London Assembly. 2018. 'Estate Regeneration'. https://www.london.gov.uk/what-we-do/housing-and-land/improving-quality/estate-regeneration. Accessed 1 August 2019.
16. The summary of the responses and the people who participated is available on the GLA website: Mayor of London. 2018. 'The Mayor's Draft Good Practice Guide to Estate Regeneration: Consultation Summary Report'. https://www.london.gov.uk/sites/default/files/draft-good-practice-guide-to-estate-regeneration-main-consultation-summary-report.pdf. Accessed 30 November 2019. Some groups have published their responses on their websites. Just Space has a list of responses from different groups: Just Space. 2017. 'Estate Regeneration: Start Again'. https://justspace.org.uk/2017/03/14/estate-regeneration-start-again/. Accessed 30 November 2019.

17. Collective response coordinated by Loretta Lees: Just Space. 2017. 'Collective Feedback from Round Table Discussion of the GLA's Recent Draft Good Practice Guide to Estate Regeneration'. https://justspacelondon.files.wordpress.com/2017/03/professor-loretta-lees-gla-draft-guidance-council-estates-feedback.pdf. Accessed 1 August 2019.
18. UCL Engineering Exchange. 2017. 'Demolition or Refurbishment of Social Housing?' https://www.ucl.ac.uk/engineering-exchange/research-projects/2019/apr/demolition-or-refurbishment-social-housing. Accessed 1 August 2019.
19. Mayor of London. 2018. *Better Homes for Local People – The Mayor's Good Practice Guide to Estate Regeneration*. London: Greater London Authority, 10.
20. Rose Grayston. 2017. *Slipping Through the Loophole: How Viability Assessments are Reducing Affordable Housing Supply in England*. London: Shelter.
21. Collective response coordinated by Loretta Lees, 'Collective Feedback from Round Table Discussion of the GLA's Recent Draft Good Practice Guide to Estate Regeneration'.
22. Collective response coordinated by Loretta Lees, 'Collective Feedback from Round Table Discussion of the GLA's Recent Draft Good Practice Guide to Estate Regeneration'.
23. These comments were drawn from the collective response coordinated by Loretta Lees, 'Collective Feedback from Round Table Discussion of the GLA's Recent Draft Good Practice Guide to Estate Regeneration'.
24. Greater London Authority. 2019. 'GLA Capital Funding Guide: Section 8: Resident Ballots for Estate Regeneration Projects'. https://www.london.gov.uk/sites/default/files/15_section_8._resident_ballots_clean_feb_2019-2.pdf. Accessed 1 August 2019.
25. Just Space. 2017. 'Draft Good Practice Guide to Estate Regeneration – Mayor of London: Response by Just Space'. https://justspacelondon.files.wordpress.com/2017/03/js-response-on-estate-regeneration-march-2017.pdf. Accessed 1 August 2019.
26. Demolition Watch through Change.org. 2016. 'Votes for Residents on Estates Facing Regeneration'. https://www.change.org/p/sadiq-khan-votes-for-residents-on-estates-facing-regeneration-e38816c6-4a5f-4405-b9b4-bedd946eb9f6. Accessed 1 August 2019.
27. Mayor of London, London Assembly. 2018. 'FOI – Estate Regeneration Schemes in London'. March 2018. https://www.london.gov.uk/about-us/governance-and-spending/sharing-our-information/freedom-information/foi-disclosure-log/foi-estate-regeneration-schemes-london. Accessed 1 August 2019.
28. Greater London Authority. 'GLA Capital Funding Guide: Section 8: Resident Ballots for Estate Regenerationprojects'. https://www.london.gov.uk/sites/default/files/15_section_8._resident_ballots_clean_feb_2019-2.pdf. Accessed 1 August 2019.
29. Greater London Authority. 'GLA Capital Funding Guide: Section 8: Resident Ballots for Estate RegenerationProjects'. https://www.london.gov.uk/sites/default/files/15_section_8._resident_ballots_clean_feb_2019-2.pdf. Accessed 1 August 2019.
30. Greater London Authority, 'GLA Capital Funding Guide: Section 8: Resident Ballots for Estate Regeneration Projects'. https://www.london.gov.uk/sites/default/files/15_section_8._resident_ballots_clean_feb_2019-2.pdf. Accessed 1 August 2019.
31. Greater London Authority, 'GLA Capital Funding Guide: Section 8: Resident Ballots for Estate Regeneration Projects', 6. https://www.london.gov.uk/sites/default/files/15_section_8._resident_ballots_clean_feb_2019-2.pdf. Accessed 1 August 2019.
32. Greater London Authority, 'GLA Capital Funding Guide: Section 8: Resident Ballots for Estate Regeneration Projects', 6. https://www.london.gov.uk/sites/default/files/15_section_8._resident_ballots_clean_feb_2019-2.pdf. Accessed 1 August 2019.
33. This section builds on work done during the Civic Design CPD Course during 2019 at The Bartlett School of Planning, UCL. The course was coordinated by Pablo Sendra, with Granville Community Kitchen and CivicWise as collaborators. The participants on the course who worked on this are Aggie Morris, Alice Devenyns, Cecilia Colombo, Dolors Vila, Dominic Cort, Iacovos Loizou, Irene Manzini Ceinar, Leslie Barson and Ursula Wyss.

11
Using the law and challenging redevelopment through the courts

Sarah Sackman[1]

How the law can help communities experiencing regeneration

Law is a critical resource in ensuring fair decision-making. It can also play a key role in shaping communities and the built environment we want to see. Communities affected by regeneration and housing campaigners working in this field need to be aware of their legal rights, and how to enforce them, in order to participate in the planning process. Decision-makers are under a host of legal duties – for example, to consult the public, to provide reasons for their decisions and to reach those decisions in a reasonable and transparent way. We know, however, that public bodies often fail to discharge those duties. Every aspect of the regeneration process – from accessing environmental information to tenants' rights to be consulted through to land acquisition and development control – is governed by legal rules which must be followed. It is vital, therefore, that communities and individuals alike are able to understand those rules, so they can seek redress where public bodies take unlawful or unfair decisions.[2]

The law can assist communities affected by regeneration plans or schemes in two broad ways. First, legal advice can help communities inform and shape plan-making and decision-taking. Using the law in this way can help to resolve residents' concerns and prevent future disputes arising. The planning system, in theory, offers many opportunities for communities to make their voices heard – for example, through public consultations, at Local Plan examinations or by attending planning inquiries or hearings on development proposals.[3] However, whether community voices are effective can depend on how residents' arguments are framed. Very often the community's concerns need to be presented in legal terms to be heard. Legal support can be vital in navigating consultations and quasi-judicial processes. Reinforcing political or policy arguments with legal advice can thus add authority to community campaigns. As illustrated in the case studies below, when deployed effectively the combination of legal advice and community organising can have a constructive impact on shaping the plans of developers, housing bodies and planning authorities alike.

The second way in which the law can be used in this context is in directly challenging public authorities' unlawful decisions. Litigation of this sort usually takes the form of a Judicial Review or 'JR'. This chapter focuses primarily on Judicial Review as a tool for challenging redevelopment. It looks at the nature of Judicial Review, the procedure for bringing a claim and ways of funding a claim. It also provides examples of where communities have successfully used this tool in the regeneration context.

In addition, the role that law and litigation can play in mobilising and creating community and housing campaigns is underappreciated. In my experience, bringing a legal challenge can become a focus for mobilising people, empowering communities and attracting local – and even national – attention on the issues raised by social housing regeneration. By involving residents in identifying the grounds of challenge, in preparing supporting evidence and in supporting a claim financially or by attending court, the law can create community and solidarity. It can also be a powerful force in helping people to shape decisions and, in some cases, to resist unwanted development.

What is Judicial Review?

Judicial Review is a procedure by which a person or group which has been affected by a decision, action or failure to act of a public body (or a body exercising a 'public function') may challenge that decision in the High Court on the basis that the body has acted unlawfully.[4] Public bodies such as central and local government have to obey the law in how they take decisions. Where they fail to, they have acted unlawfully. Judicial Review is concerned not with the merits of the decision (e.g. whether the proposed development is good or bad), but only with whether the public body has acted lawfully.

In the regeneration context, Judicial Review challenges will be to decisions of the local authority or the Secretary of State (usually through one of their appointed planning inspectors).[5] A Judicial Review may be brought by an individual or by a group affected by the decision in question.

A public authority may be acting unlawfully if it has made a decision or done something:

- without the legal power to do so **(illegality)**.
- so unreasonable that no reasonable decision-maker could have come to the same decision or done the same thing **(irrationality)**. This could be because a decision-maker has taken into account an irrelevant consideration or failed to have regard to a relevant consideration.
- without observing the rules of natural justice **(procedural impropriety)**. Examples of procedural unfairness include biased decision-making, a failure to consult, a failure to give reasons for a decision or the breach of legitimate expectation that something would happen based on a promise made or practice adopted by the authority.
- in breach of European Community Law or the Human Rights Act 1998.
- in breach of Public Sector Equality Duty.[6]

These grounds are neither exhaustive nor mutually exclusive. A claim may be brought on multiple grounds.

What can the court do?

If one of these grounds of challenge is made out and the court finds that the public authority has acted unlawfully, it can grant a remedy including:

- a mandatory order (i.e. an order requiring the public body to do something)
- a prohibiting order (i.e. an order preventing the public body from doing something)
- a quashing order (i.e. an order quashing the public body's decision)
- a declaration
- (in rare cases) award damages.

A successful Judicial Review will often result in the quashing of the decision under challenge. For example, a successful Judicial Review of a decision to grant planning permission for the redevelopment of an estate will usually mean the planning permission is cancelled and the matter is remitted to the decision-making body for reconsideration.

However, it is important to understand that Judicial Review remedies are discretionary. This means that even if a claimant is able to show that a decision-maker has acted improperly, the court may decline to grant the remedy sought if, for example, it considers that even without the legal error it is highly likely the decision would have been the same.[7]

Moreover, even if a Judicial Review is successful and a remedy is granted, that will not necessarily result in a different outcome from the original decision. Where, for example, the Judicial Review succeeds on the basis of a procedural defect, such as failure to consult, it is possible that, following proper consultation, the same decision will be reached. Campaigners considering bringing a claim will therefore need to balance the potentially powerful Judicial Review remedies – which can stop unwanted development going ahead or compel the public body to involve local people – against the inherent uncertainty of outcome.

When to bring a Judicial Review?

Time limits for bringing a Judicial Review are tight, and especially so in planning cases. Challenges to the grant of planning permission or the adoption of local development plans must be made within six weeks of the decision. For other types of decisions, for example the failure to consult on a decision to set up a local authority development vehicle or a new development strategy, claimants are required to bring a Judicial Review 'promptly' and within three months of the decision under challenge.[8]

These time limits are strictly enforced, so it is necessary to act promptly. Even though the periods for challenging decisions are short, planning decisions often comprise several stages and can have long lead-in times – for example, from the time a planning application is submitted to its final determination. Given that, as soon as you become aware of redevelopment plans or proposals, you should identify sources of legal and professional support. In practice, it can take several weeks to gather the necessary information to ascertain whether you have a strong legal claim, so the sooner you seek advice the better.

Finally, where decision-making takes place in stages, deciding which decision to challenge can assume tactical importance for your litigation and campaign strategy. You will need to assess the implications of challenging a decision early in the regeneration process as opposed to waiting until proposals have become more fully developed.

What is the procedure for applying for a Judicial Review?

Applying for Judicial Review is a multi-staged process. Below we set out each of the stages that a claim may go through, from the exchange of pre-action correspondence to a final hearing in court.

Pre-action stage

Where you consider the public body has acted unlawfully, you should write to them setting out why, expressing the intention to apply for Judicial Review and asking them to rectify the situation. That letter is called a 'pre-action protocol letter'. It is a critical document and should be prepared, if possible, by a lawyer. Many public authorities may withdraw a disputed decision or agree to take remedial steps in response to a well-crafted letter. A pre-action letter can also lead to obtaining disclosure of critical matters.

On the other hand, a well-drafted response from the public body can help potential claimants by highlighting weaknesses in their arguments which can help refine a claim or inform the decision about whether a case is strong enough to bring to court. The pre-action stage does not carry the costs risks of formal proceedings, discussed below.

Many campaigners have found that public bodies who may have been dismissive of their voices before obtaining legal help suddenly sit up and take notice if they think they may face a legal challenge. Pre-action letters are therefore not only an important part of the Judicial Review protocol, but may themselves be important campaigning tools.

Issuing the claim

If you do not get a satisfactory response to your letter, the next step is to apply for Judicial Review. Together with your legal team (usually a solicitor and a barrister), you will need to prepare a written statement of facts and grounds and submit any evidence on which you intend to rely. The public body – referred to at this stage as the 'defendant' – and any interested parties – for example, a developer or housing association – is then given 21 days from when they receive your claim to file an acknowledgement of service and set out their response to the claim. The claim must be issued within the time limits set out above.

Permission stage

All the papers are then put before a judge who decides whether to grant permission for the claim to proceed to a full hearing. To obtain permission, you will need to persuade a judge that your case is arguable. If permission is refused, you have seven days to ask the court to reconsider the claim at an oral hearing. If permission is again refused, an application can be made to the Court of Appeal. If permission is refused once more, that is the end of the case.

Full hearing

If permission to apply for Judicial Review is granted, the case will go to a full hearing. The various parties will then be asked to prepare and serve detailed grounds, evidence and written arguments.

The hearing is very formal. It is unlikely that there will be any oral evidence and the case will revolve around hearing legal arguments from the lawyers. In most cases, at the end of the hearing, the judge will 'reserve' judgement, meaning that the judgement will be given in writing at a later date, usually several weeks after the hearing itself. Once judgement has been given, both sides can make representations about who should pay the costs of the proceedings.

While there is no fixed time frame for a Judicial Review, the whole process from start to finish can take around six months or longer. If the matter is urgent, it is possible to apply for the claim to be expedited and decided more quickly. Additionally, parties may apply to the court for an order that the regeneration process be halted while the Judicial Review claim is pending (this is referred to as an injunction).

The duration of a Judicial Review has important consequences for community groups and campaigners. If the Judicial Review results in delaying the regeneration process, that can lead local authorities or developers to modify their plans. On the other hand, delay can produce hardship for some sections of the community if it postpones necessary works or affects the relocation and compensation of individuals who do wish to move. It is therefore important to think through the potential consequences of a Judicial Review and its timing for all those involved.

When we recommend using this tool

It is important to recognise some of the challenges of bringing a Judicial Review:

- **The cost**: Judicial Review can be expensive, although not as expensive as many people think (see below, 'Technical and financial support'). Claimants will need to pay their own lawyers, and if you lose you will normally have to pay the other side's legal costs. All of those costs must be considered before commencing a claim.
- **The risk**: Even if a court finds that a public body has acted unlawfully, it may decide not to set aside the decision being challenged. This is because, as explained, the remedies in Judicial Review are at the court's discretion. Legal experts can advise in advance on the prospects of success, but there is no such thing as a 'sure win' in Judicial Review.
- **The complexity**: The law, derived from legislation and case law, as well as the technical evidence which may be involved in regeneration cases – for example, on viability or environmental impacts – mean that specialist legal input is essential.

So how should a group decide whether this is an appropriate route for them? Judicial Review should be viewed as a remedy of last resort. Where you consider the public authority has acted unlawfully, you need to consider whether you have exhausted any alternative avenues of redress – such as a complaints procedure – before resorting to Judicial Review. In practical terms, the threat of bringing a Judicial Review may be considered a 'nuclear' option. If, for example, you or your group have been working closely and co-operatively with the local planning authority, the threat of legal action may irrevocably change that relationship.

However, if you consider that local voices are being ignored and that decisions are not being fairly or lawfully taken, Judicial Review can be a powerful tool – sometimes the only one available – for challenging the regeneration process. As the case studies illustrate, the use of legal argument and Judicial Review can be extremely effective in holding public bodies to account, securing a voice for local people and setting a legal precedent.

Technical and financial support

Individuals and groups wishing to bring a Judicial Review naturally worry about the costs involved. However, there are plenty of sources of support available. You must budget for two main items of expenditure:

- the cost of paying your own legal representatives (which are likely to be paid by the other side if you win)
- the other side's costs (which you are likely to have to pay if your challenge is unsuccessful). As noted above, if you win the other side is likely to have to pay your legal costs.

The usual rule in Judicial Review is that costs follow the event, meaning that the loser of a Judicial Review is ordered to pay the winner's costs. You may be able to agree a fixed fee with your own lawyers, but you will not know the other side's costs in advance. The cost of running a Judicial Review from start to finish can cost in the region of £30,000. However, there are a number of ways to reduce and remove the financial barriers to litigation:

- **Legal aid**: In certain cases, individuals may be eligible for legal aid funding. Applicants for legal aid will have to meet the eligibility requirements and demonstrate they are of limited means, as well as having a meritorious claim. In practice, even when a potential claimant is eligible for legal aid it can take considerable time to put this in place, and a community contribution may be required.
- **Costs caps**: The EU's Aarhus Convention[9] confers on individuals the rights to public participation and access to environmental justice. It has had a significant impact on our legal system in preventing claims from becoming prohibitively expensive. Most notably, it has led to the introduction of costs caps. In most cases a Judicial Review in the regeneration context will be treated as an 'environmental' or 'Aarhus' claim, meaning that it is likely to be subject to a costs cap. This means that a claimant's costs liability is capped from the start of the litigation, so that they know, for certain, how much they will have to pay to the other side in the event that the claim is unsuccessful. The default costs caps under the Civil Procedure Rules are £5000 for an individual or £10,000 for a group.[10] This means that if you bring an environmental claim in your name, you will not be liable to the other side for more than £5000 in costs, i.e. that is the most you will have to pay the other side if you lose (in addition to paying your own legal representatives).

- **Crowdfunding**: Increasing numbers of public interest environmental/regeneration claims are funded through crowdfunding procedures, which seek to raise money through donations from the community and wider public. There are a number of crowdfunding platforms that support this form of fundraising.[11] Crowdfunding for litigation can be a site of mobilisation for community groups, as well as a chance to reach and attract the 'buy-in' of the wider public in cases raising issues in the public interest.
- *Pro bono* **representation**: There are a number of organisations, charities and community-based law centres that provide free advice and, in some cases, *pro bono* representation in Judicial Review.[12] However, this does not protect you from the costs risk of having to pay the other side's costs if you lose.
- **Conditional or discounted fee agreements**: It is critical to engage specialist lawyers with experience of public and planning law. Some lawyers may agree to act for you under a conditional/discounted fee agreement. This is sometimes referred to as a 'no win, no fee' arrangement. This means that your solicitor or barrister will not charge any fees or will not charge their full fees unless you win your case. You will still need to be protected against having to pay the other side's costs (see 'Costs caps' above). Most lawyers will prefer to work under an agreed conditional/discounted fee rather than *pro bono*, as there is a chance they will get paid in full (out of the other side's costs) if the case is successful.

Case study 1: Equalities law and regeneration, Foxhill Estate, Bath

The Foxhill estate consisted of 500 homes, mainly council houses, and was earmarked for regeneration. Residents had sought to resist the regeneration plans for several years, forming the Foxhill Residents' Association and lobbying Bath and North East Somerset Council to consider refurbishment of the estate rather than its redevelopment. Eventually, the council granted planning permission to the housing association responsible for the estate to demolish the Foxhill estate completely and redevelop it. The proposal re-provided 700 mainly market rent homes, with the net loss of over 200 council houses.

Peter Buckley, a Foxhill resident, sought legal advice and issued a Judicial Review of the planning permission. I represented Mr Buckley. We argued, among other things, that the council had not discharged its

Public Sector Equality Duty (PSED) under section 149 of the Equality Act 2010.[13] That duty requires public bodies in the exercise of their public functions to have due regard to the impacts of their decisions on persons with protected characteristics (including by virtue of their race, sex, sexuality, age, disability and religion). We argued that the council's Planning Committee had not been provided with information, and therefore had failed to consider the impact of the redevelopment and the forced displacement, in particular, on elderly and disabled residents. Had they had due regard for this, their decision might have been different.

Mr Buckley funded his claim through crowdfunding and obtained a costs cap, by agreement with the council, which limited his costs exposure to £2000. His claim succeeded on the basis that the council had failed to discharge its PSED; the court ordered that the planning permission be quashed and that the council pay Mr Buckley's costs.[14] The judgement received extensive coverage in the press.[15] The developer housing association subsequently decided to withdraw its planning application and is now refurbishing the estate. As well as securing a successful result for Foxhill residents, the case set a national precedent that the PSED and equalities considerations apply to all development decisions, and particularly in the context of estate regeneration.

Case study 2: Fair consultation of residents, Cressingham Gardens

Planning authorities are required to consult residents on plans and on planning applications which may affect their estates. The obligation to consult may arise due to a specific statutory requirement or as a matter of fairness. If a planning authority fails to consult, or fails to carry out that consultation properly, it can give rise to grounds for Judicial Review.

The courts have laid the criteria (known as the Principles of Fair Consultation)[16] that all fair public consultations must satisfy, namely that:

- consultation must be at a time when proposals are at a formative stage
- sufficient reasons must be given for any proposal to allow an intelligent consideration of and response to the proposal
- adequate time must be given for the consideration and response
- responses must be conscientiously taken into account in any final decision.

In a case about reductions in council tax support,[17] for example, the Supreme Court considered the extent to which a decision-maker is required to provide information on options that have been considered but not pursued, and the reasons why such options have been discarded. The court indicated that in some cases fairness will require that interested persons be consulted not only upon the preferred option, but also upon available, yet discarded, alternative options. This is potentially important in the context of estate regeneration where different options are being explored. The court underscored the constitutional value of involving the public in the decision-making process. It specifically underlined that where the affected members of the public are economically disadvantaged, those people should be given more specific information about proposals.

A notable example of a challenge to a consultation in the regeneration context arose in relation to Cressingham Gardens (see chapter 3). As part of a wider campaign, a tenant of Cressingham Gardens applied for Judicial Review of Lambeth's decision to redevelop rather than refurbish the estate.[18] The council was required under section 105 of the Housing Act 1985 to inform and consult residents on matters relating to housing management. Having announced that it would consult on five options, including refurbishment as well as redevelopment options, the council later dropped the refurbishment options, saying that these would be too costly. The High Court found there was no legitimate basis for the council to stop consulting on all of the options after it had promised to do so. The effect of the Judicial Review was that the decision to redevelop the estate was quashed. Lambeth later retook its decision to redevelop Cressingham Gardens. Due to this claim and another unsuccessful Judicial Review,[19] the redevelopment of the estate has been delayed. See chapter 3 on Cressingham Gardens for an update on the situation and other strategies used by residents.

Case study 3: Community influence in plan-making, the draft London Plan

Planning authorities are required to produce, and keep under review, planning documents which set the policy framework for their areas, including for social housing regeneration. The public should be involved in this process. Given that plans can establish the principle of regeneration of an estate, community engagement[20] at all stages of the plan-making process, including consultation responses[21] and attendance at the public examination of the draft plan, is vital. If communities do not get involved at this stage, it can mean that when specific development proposals come forward they are more difficult to resist because the principle of regeneration has already been set in the plan.

However, community groups rarely get involved in the plan-making process; often that is because they do not know they can. This is an important missed opportunity as communities can try to influence the substance of the policies that will affect them for years to come.[22] Obtaining legal advice on how best to navigate this process can be of real assistance.

Just Space – the London-wide network of community groups – has engaged extensively over the years on the preparation of the draft London Plan, to great effect.[23] In 2019 Just Space made representations through its members in writing and orally at the Examination in Public on a wide range of policy matters, from the use of industrial sites to social infrastructure and social housing regeneration. Just Space suggested specific changes to the text and approach of the plan, and some of these points are likely to be reflected in the final version, which will be published by March 2020.

In developing its responses Just Space sought legal advice on whether the draft London Plan complied with the legal requirements under the Equality Act 2010. Just Space argued that the Mayor's Integrated Impact Assessment, published with the draft Plan, did not discharge this duty under the PSED. In particular, Just Space argued that the impact assessment failed to examine the draft Plan's specific impacts – both negative and positive – on protected groups such as black, Asian and minority ethnic and disabled people, including in the context of estate regeneration.[24]

As a result of Just Space's intervention, the Mayor was directed by the Examination Panel to publish his underlying evidence base and equalities data. The GLA was asked to explain how they had taken into account different impacts on protected groups, which the draft Plan had failed to do in the original impact assessment. The Mayor's team produced a report justifying its approach to equalities considerations. This would not have happened without Just Space's intervention. The outcome exemplifies how legal and policy arguments can hold public bodies to account and can influence the substance of plans.

Conclusion

Judicial Review challenges brought by communities have the potential to make a powerful impact in those communities and well beyond. Due to our common law system, a principle established in one case can have ramifications in other cases – and for other estates – where that precedent is applied. By challenging a council on its process and approach to decision-making, such claims can have a corrective effect on public bodies' practices and behaviour in respect of future regeneration schemes. A challenge, say, to the failure to discharge the PSED in one case can lead that public body, and more wary others, to improve their policies and culture in respect of equalities, thus reducing the risk of future breaches.

Using the law in this way is an important tool. It is sometimes the only means of resisting unwanted and unlawful development. In addition, the role that Judicial Review can play in mobilising a campaign, formalising it and providing a focus and forum in which the residents' voices are heard by the courts, and by decision-makers, is underappreciated. Taking legal advice and obtaining legal representation can be empowering for community campaigners. Simply knowing your rights to participate, and the ways in which those can be enforced, can mean that representations are sharper, more focused and more effective – producing better outcomes and genuine community-led regeneration.

Notes

1. Barrister, Francis Taylor Building, Inner Temple. Visiting Lecturer at LSE Cities Programme. sarah.sackman@ftbchambers.co.uk.
2. This chapter is intended for information only and is not legal advice. While we hope it will be helpful to those involved in or considering Judicial Review, it is not a replacement for legal advice. If you believe you have a case, you should seek specialist legal advice immediately.
3. The Planning Inspectorate provides guidance and explanatory videos on public participation in planning inquiries. The Planning Inspectorate. September 2019. 'Guide to Taking Part in Planning and Listed Building Consent Appeals Proceeding by an Inquiry – England'. https://assets.publishing.service.gov.uk/government/uploads/system/uploads/attachment_data/file/832054/taking-part_planning-inquiry_September_2019.pdf. Accessed 16 October 2019.
4. For a general user-friendly introduction to the subject, see Public Law Project. 6 February 2019. 'An Introduction to Judicial Review'. https://publiclawproject.org.uk/resources/an-introduction-to-judicial-review-2/. Accessed 16 October 2019.
5. In challenges to the grant of planning permission, there are generally only two parties involved: the developer making the application and the local planning authority deciding whether or not to grant planning permission. Communities and individuals are regarded as third parties and do not have a right to appeal. As such, Judicial Review provides the only opportunity for further action once a decision to approve development has been made by a local authority.
6. Equality Act 2010, Section 149: Public Sector Equality Duty. http://www.legislation.gov.uk/ukpga/2010/15/section/149. Accessed 16 October 2019.
7. Under section 31 of the Senior Courts Act 1981, if the public authority is able to show that it was highly likely that the outcome for the claimant would not have been substantially different had the authority acted lawfully, the court may withhold relief and refuse to quash the decision. Senior Court Act 1981, Section 31: Application for Judicial Review. http://www.legislation.gov.uk/ukpga/1981/54/section/31. Accessed 16 October 2019.
8. Civil Procedure Rules, Part 54: Judicial Review and Statutory Review. https://www.justice.gov.uk/courts/procedure-rules/civil/rules/part54. Accessed 16 October 2019.

9. UNECE Convention on Access to Information, Public Participation in Decision-Making and Access to Justice in Environmental Matters (Aarhus Convention, 1998). https://www.unece.org/fileadmin/DAM/env/pp/documents/cep43e.pdf. Accessed 16 October 2019.

10. Civil Procedure Rule 45.43: Civil Procedure Rule, Part 45: Fixed Costs. https://www.justice.gov.uk/courts/procedure-rules/civil/rules/part45-fixed-costs. Accessed 16 October 2019.

11. See, for example, Crowdjustice. https://www.crowdjustice.com/. Accessed 16 October 2019.

12. See, for example, the Environmental Law Foundation. https://elflaw.org/. Accessed 16 October 2019; Bar Pro Bono Unit/Advocate. https://weareadvocate.org.uk/. Accessed 16 October 2019.

13. The claim was funded through crowdfunding and benefited from an agreed costs cap.

14. *R (Buckley) v Bath and North East Somerset Council & Anor* [2018]. EWHC 1551 (Admin) (20 June 2018). http://www.bailii.org/ew/cases/EWHC/Admin/2018/1551.html. Accessed 16 October 2019.

15. Amanda Cameron. 20 June 2018. 'Victory for Foxhill Residents as Judge Quashes Approval of Curo's Plans for Demolition – Live Updates'. *SomersetLive*. https://www.somersetlive.co.uk/in-your-area/victory-foxhill-residents-after-judge-1695031. Accessed 16 October 2019.

16. Sometimes known as the Sedley Principles after the judge in the case *R v Brent London Borough Council, ex. p. Gunning* [1985]. 84 LGR 168.

17. *R (Moseley)* v London Borough of Haringey [2014] UKSC 56 (29 October 2014). http://www.bailii.org/uk/cases/UKSC/2014/56.html. Accessed 26 October 2019.

18. *R (Bokrosova) v London Borough of Lambeth* [2015] EWHC 3386 (Admin). http://www.bailii.org/ew/cases/EWHC/Admin/2015/3386.html. Accessed 23 January 2020.

19. A further *R (Plant) v Lambeth LBC*[2017] PTSR 453. http://www.bailii.org/ew/cases/EWHC/Admin/2016/3324.html. Accessed 27 January 2020.

20. The local planning authority must comply with its statement of community involvement: Section 19(3) Planning and Compulsory Purchase Act 2004. Planning and Compulsory Purchase Act 2004, Section 19: Preparation of local development documents. http://www.legislation.gov.uk/ukpga/2004/5/section/19. Accessed 26 October 2019.

21. Local planning authorities are required to consult the public on at least two occasions on their draft Local Plan. See Regulations 18 and 19, Town and Country Planning (Local Planning) Regulations 2012. http://www.legislation.gov.uk/uksi/2012/767/contents/made. Accessed 26 October 2019.

22. Another important way in which groups can influence Local Plan-making includes neighbourhood planning under the Localism Act 2011.

23. At the time of writing (October 2019) the draft London Plan had gone through planning examination.

24. Draft policy H10 of the London Plan (for Just Space's full representations see https://justspace.org.uk/).

12
Informal tools and strategies

None of the campaigns and groups discussed in the first part of this book have relied solely on formal planning frameworks and tools. The case studies show that, in addition to a formal engagement with planning, it is essential that a campaign or group of residents employ other tools and strategies outside formal planning. This is mainly because informal actions, strategies and tools provide more flexibility, can adapt better to the timing needed by the community (rather than the community having to adapt to the timing of a planning framework) and can have an effect in the short term. They can also build a path towards (or support) other strategies that require formal engagement with planning.

This chapter has two parts. The first will discuss an informal planning tool that has been used by four of the seven case studies presented – the People's Plan (also named community plan or alternative community-led plan). A People's Plan is a vision for the neighbourhood that has been put together by residents in collaboration with architects, planners and/or other professionals hired by the residents. A People's Plan is not statutory (unlike a Neighbourhood Plan). However, in some situations, a People's Plan has been used in coordination with, or as additional evidence for, supporting the use of a formal planning tool or framework. A People's Plan can, in short, be used as a tool to oppose demolition and propose an alternative plan.

The second part of the chapter presents a list of actions, strategies and campaigning tools that residents can use to oppose demolition and propose alternative plans. This provides a brief catalogue for campaigning, on which future campaigners can build and extend. These actions, strategies and tools should also be used in coordination with others for, as the case studies have shown, strategies are less effective in isolation.

The People's Plan

When residents see that their neighbourhood is under threat of demolition and they may face displacement, they can decide to come together and draft their own alternative plan. This brings together their vision for the neighbourhood and moves them as a group from the oppositional to a propositional platform. On many occasions, residents hire architects, planners and/or other professionals to assist them in the preparation of the People's Plan. In the case studies discussed, such collaboration with professionals has been achieved in different ways. For example, the Cressingham Gardens and the West Kensington and Gibbs Green (WKGG) communities hired an architectural practice (Variant Office and Architects for Social Housing respectively) to draft the People's Plan; they also used other consultants to produce the evidence-based documents that support the People's Plan. The common practice is for residents to organise events such as meetings, walks through the neighbourhood, co-design events and discussions with residents for developing together a shared vision. Thus the residents serve as the clients of the architects, who have to address these multiple voices in the context of a coherent vision.

In the case of People's Empowerment Alliance for Custom House (PEACH), the community group put together their own in-house team by hiring individual architects and community organisers to form a team and to work on a community-led plan. In this case the team organised a series of workshops and also had regular meetings with their Housing Club, the group within PEACH that deals with issues concerning regeneration. In other cases, such as the Carpenters Estate, the production of the People's Plan was undertaken with the support of external organisations (London Tenants Federation (LTF) and Just Space, with a grant from the journal *Antipode*), voluntary postgraduate (MSc and PhD) students from UCL (the collaboration being coordinated by Just Space) and other LTF members.[1]

People's Plans have a long history and existed before the recent wave of social housing demolition associated with the period of austerity. Planners' Network UK used to have a wiki website where people could contribute references, links and relevant historical background on People's Plans. The website is no longer active, but Michael Edwards has a copy of it on his blog.[2] Here the importance of campaigns such as the Covent Garden Community Association in the 1970s is presented.[3] This campaign played a key role in stopping a large-scale urban development that would have transformed Covent Garden into a motorway surrounded by office blocks. The blog also presents the history of the Coin Street Community Builders, an organisation that grew from the Coin Street Action Group. This group, created in response to proposed office and hotel development, successfully campaigned for a community-led housing development in the late 1970s/early 1980s.[4] The Coin Street Community Builders eventually managed to acquire 13 acres of land in 1984 for their community-led development.[5]

Usefulness for community-led regeneration

The People's Plan is one of the most effective tools that residents can use to oppose demolition and propose an alternative plan. The main reason for its strength is because it demonstrates that the residents have a shared vision of how they would like their neighbourhood to be. It demonstrates that residents are not just opposing redevelopment plans, but that they also propose alternative options for improving the neighbourhood.

We present the People's Plan as an 'informal tool' because it is not statutory, and thus the plan itself (without being combined with other strategies) is not legally binding. When the community produces a People's Plan, subsequent developments – either private or public – are not obliged to follow it.

The preparation of a People's Plan follows a similar process to producing a formal masterplan. However, it provides more flexibility and residents have control over the timing and decision-making process of the project. The residents act as clients and the professionals or volunteers involved facilitate a co-design process through workshops, events, consultations, surveys, discussions, meetings, walks through the neighbourhood and other engagement methods. Since the residents are the clients and are directly hiring the professionals, they can determine the timing of the process and discuss the project until they are satisfied with it; they also have much more flexibility to produce the plan.

Although a People's Plan is not statutory, it can have a legal effect when combined with other forms of formal engagement with planning. In the case of Cressingham Gardens, the People's Plan and its supporting documents have been instrumental in successfully getting the Ministry of Housing, Communities and Local Government to support their Right to Transfer. The fact that the group could prove that their option was viable, and that they had the ability to supply social housing, made their case much stronger.

The case studies have shown that a People's Plan can be used in different situations. In the case of Carpenters Estate, the residents, with the support of other organisations and volunteers, put together a community plan at the early stages of their campaign. The creation of this plan built the path for the formation of the Neighbourhood Forum (NF) and the elaboration of a Neighbourhood Plan (NP) under the regulations of the Localism Act 2011 (as discussed in chapter 9). The Neighbourhood Plan was submitted six years after the community plan. However, doing a community plan or People's Plan before the neighbourhood plan offered two major advantages. First, an evidence-based community-led plan was developed in a short period of time without the need of going through the lengthy process of neighbourhood planning. Second, by producing a People's Plan, the community developed their own capacity for putting together the subsequent, more formal Neighbourhood Plan.

In the case of PEACH, the production of their community-led plan provided them with the possibility of negotiating with the local authority and becoming partners in the regeneration of the area, as discussed in chapter 6.

In the cases of Cressingham Gardens Community and West Ken Gibbs Green Community Homes (WKGGCH), the People's Plan, in addition to providing a community vision, also aimed to support their case for the Right to Transfer. In this instance, the 'informal' tool was used in combination with other formal planning strategies.

Difficulties found and how to overcome them

One of the difficulties encountered, since a People's Plan is not statutory, is that the council, housing associations and developers can disregard the plan. However, councils have the legal obligation to undertake a consultation (see chapter 11); on this basis, communities that produce a People's Plan should require local authorities to consider it. In order to strengthen the plan, the support of evidence-based documents is important. These should include both quantitative and qualitative information on how the consultation and the engagement process have been carried out and how many people have participated. It is also important to provide technical evidence supporting the plan and to include a financial viability assessment.

Another strategy to overcome the fact that the plan is not considered a statutory document is to produce a People's Plan in conjunction with some formal planning tools. As the case studies have shown, the

People's Plan can be used either to request the local authority to join in a formal partnership or participate in the regeneration process, or to use it as a supporting document for other formal planning tools, such as the Right to Transfer.

Another difficulty that communities may encounter – although to our knowledge, this has not occurred in any of the case studies discussed here – is a lack of agreement between the different members of the community regarding a shared vision for the neighbourhood. In such cases the appointment of an external planner, community organiser or other mediator who can act as a facilitator can help to consolidate a shared and coherent vision.

Last but not least is the difficulty of raising funds to pay for the necessary technical support for putting together a People's Plan. This is discussed below in the 'Technical and financial support available' section.

When we recommend to use this tool

Residents concerned with the plans of a council, housing association and/or developer for demolishing and redeveloping their neighbourhood can use People's Plans as an effective tool to oppose these plans and offer an alternative vision. In particular, residents should consider putting together a People's Plan when they feel that the council, housing association and/or developer is not sensitive to their concerns (which includes being aware of, but not considering, their views on the plans).

While councils, housing associations and developers may carry out a consultation process and subsequently promise rehousing arrangements or a right to return, it is very important to scrutinise such consultation processes and ensure that they are lawfully conducted (see chapter 11). In addition, any offers of rehousing and right to return options need to be examined carefully to make sure that residents are fully aware of the associated conditions. The anti-gentrification handbook *Staying Put*, prepared in 2014 by the London Tenants Federation, Loretta Lees, Just Space and Southwark Notes Archive Group, explains the problems with consultation processes in which residents do not have the chance to influence decision-making.[6] It also highlights the problems that the right to return had in the case of the Heygate Estate in Elephant and Castle, in the London Borough of Southwark. When councils, housing associations and/or developers approach residents with a consultation on the redevelopment of the estate, it is important that residents insist that the council consider, assess and offer refurbishment as an option.

A People's Plan is therefore a tool we particularly recommend for use in situations where groups of residents want an alternative plan to that of the council, housing association and/or developer. The reasons for strongly recommending this tool are as follows:

- It requires less time than a Neighbourhood Plan and residents have more control over the process. It is very useful to have, relatively quickly, a community vision that can be used in different ways to demand alternatives to the council's proposals.
- It does not prevent a group from preparing a Neighbourhood Plan. In fact, as the case of Carpenters Estate has shown, a People's Plan can be a first step towards a Neighbourhood Plan.
- It demonstrates the community's capacity to self-organise. In some cases, as in the case of PEACH, this may encourage the council to work in partnership with the community.
- It can be used to support other formal planning tools such as the Right to Transfer.
- It can be used at different stages of the campaign, as the case studies have demonstrated. It can be used at the beginning of resistance to bring together a community vision or much later on when it is needed for a particular purpose.

Technical and financial support available

There are no specific funding schemes for People's Plans (as there is for neighbourhood planning). However, some not-for-profit organisations have a particular interest in the exploration of community-led developments, and are funding similar initiatives. The case studies discussed in this book clearly show the source(s) of funding in their People's Plan document. In many of the cases, the groups received funding from the not-for-profit organisations that support community-led planning.

In addition to these sources, it is possible to identify particular discrete sources of funding that might promote one of the values or features of the People's Plan. These could include energy retrofit, refurbishment, fuel poverty, solar energy, community ownership, self-build, etc.

Another possibility is to organise a crowdfunding campaign to pay for the fees of professional support. A number of crowdfunding and fundraising platforms exist that can host the campaign. Note that different platforms offer different levels of support; some also charge fees (a percentage of the funds) and others do not.

Finally, another possibility is to use collaboration with volunteers and with university students (urban planning, architecture, geography, engineering). Just Space has been running an 'extra-curricular programme' for several years with UCL students. They work with community groups as well as collaborating with different MSc modules at UCL's Bartlett School of Planning, Department of Geography and Development Planning Unit,[7] where students produce work that is useful for community groups. The UCL Engineering Exchange and UCL Department of Engineering have worked with the residents of the Carpenters Estate and Just Space for proposals on infrastructure. At The Bartlett School of Planning, the Civic Design CPD course has collaborated with community groups, agreeing before the course on a brief that provides appropriate support to the community group. In the 2019 edition of the Civic Design CPD course, students produced an initial document that will help to draft a People's Plan for a group of residents faced with the demolition of their homes. In addition to such initiatives, other universities across London have funding schemes that provide support for knowledge transfer and for supporting collaboration between students, staff and communities.

Case studies using this tool

- Cressingham Gardens Community put together a People's Plan, which has a number of annex documents that provide further evidence on the financial viability of the plan and on its sustainability. The plan has been instrumental to the group's success in the Right to Transfer campaign. To develop the plan, they hired a local architect who had previously lived in the estate.
- WKGGCH, in anticipation of carrying out a feasibility study for the Right to Transfer, hired Architects for Social Housing to translate their vision into a People's Plan. The proposal consisted of refurbishment and adding between 200 and 300 homes.
- Carpenters Estate residents, with the support of LTF, Just Space, volunteers, and MSc and PhD students from UCL, put together their community plan in 2013. This community plan formed a precedent for their Neighbourhood Plan, which was submitted in June 2019.
- PEACH created their own team of architects and community organisers to draft a community-led plan in 2017. The plan has been instrumental in getting the council to create a partnership with PEACH for the regeneration of Custom House.

Actions, strategies and campaigning tools

From the seven case studies discussed in this book, we have compiled a list of actions, strategies and campaigning tools with the aim of providing some guidance for campaigns. This list is not complete, but can be extended by other campaigners and/or researchers.

Mobilising people

One of the key elements of a campaign is mobilising people for a common cause. In many of the case studies presented here, the common cause is saving their homes from demolition and improving the built environment of their neighbourhood. Getting people together and forming a campaign, a community interest group or other forms of association can be challenging, but there are strategies that can help. Some of these are discussed in Part III of this book, in the topic 'Community organising'. These strategies can include direct appeals through 'door-knocking', creating posters and leaflets and distributing them around the estate, and organising events and communal activities where residents can be informed about the situation. The physical presence of a stall, as used by Focus E15 (chapter 5), can also be a particularly effective way to advertise and engage with residents, as in some cases people do not like being approached on the doorstep or being handed a leaflet.

To carry out these activities, it is useful to have the support of a community organiser who can be hired by the residents if sufficient funds are available. If they are not, the community could approach local charities that may be interested in providing some volunteer support. Once a significant group of people has been created, it is important to reach an agreement on the shared values of the campaign and on some form of governance and decision-making protocols (see the topic 'Community organising' in Part III).

Online presence

The importance of campaigns having an online presence cannot be overstated, and the use of blogs and social media has made it quite easy for campaigns to achieve this. All campaigns and groups included in this book have their own blogs and social media accounts. The use of MySQL blog platforms, such as WordPress[8] or other free website builders, enables campaigns to have a professional-looking website with some basic

IT skills and at a very low cost (cheap or even free web-hosting sites are available). Profiles can be created in social media and blogs should always be updated with relevant information on the campaign.

Social media can also be used to advertise events, post news and interact with other campaigns, supporters, politicians and developers. During the discussion workshops in our final event (see 'Community organising' in Part III), there was some discussion on the use of social media. In these the importance of being respectful when applying pressure through social media was noted.

Applying pressure

Putting pressure on local authorities, housing associations and developers to listen to the voices of residents is a very important part of the campaign. This can be done through letter writing, sending emails, making contact with the local MP, social media, public demonstrations, and asking for an appointment with the person or the team responsible for the regeneration and the organisations involved in the redevelopment. As discussed before, it is important to be calm and respectful while applying pressure.

Graphic design, communication and activism

Graphic design and communication constitute important elements of any campaign, and leaflets and posters have to be designed in a particular way to be effective. Examples of good practice for effective graphic design and communication, bringing people together, are available. The posters and graphic material produced by Walterton and Elgin Action Group (WEAG) in their campaign for ownership of the Walterton and Elgin estates (see fig.1.1 in chapter 1), for example, had a very strong message on the threat to the neighbourhood posed by developers. In the case of Cressingham Gardens, the leaflets with the 'STOP DEMOLITION' sign also sent out a powerful message to bring everyone together for a common cause.

Direct action

Direct action has been effective in some cases where groups have forced a response from the council and developers. WEAG, for example, visited the different developers involved in purchasing their estates and managed to stop the sale. Focus E15 carried out the 'political occupation' of an empty block on the Carpenters Estate to demonstrate that the council was failing to provide social housing while keeping housing blocks that were in good condition empty. When carrying out direct action, it is important to generate support from different organisations, to be clear about the message and purpose of the action, and to be respectful to everyone.

Building alliances with other campaigns, and getting support from organisations and politicians

For campaigns, it is important to build alliances with other groups who are going through similar situations. This helps to build networks of solidarity and also to exchange knowledge regarding opposition to demolition and the proposal of community-led plans. The support of other organisations, such as universities and charities, or from politicians, is also important. Holding open events and inviting other groups and organisations also helps to build these networks of support.

Community and open events

As indicated above, community events are helpful in building the internal support for the campaign and strengthening its internal structure; they also offer useful opportunities to discuss with other residents the situation and strategies to take. Open events are important and useful to enlarge the campaign's visibility and to gain support from other organisations and individuals. We have attended open events that were clearly very successful in bringing people together. These include the theatre performance narrating the regeneration process in Cressingham Gardens in June 2016 and the film screening on community ownership in West Kensington and Gibbs Green in June 2019.

Notes

1. Greater Carpenters Community Plan. 2013. 'Carpenters Community Plan 2013'. http://www.londontenants.org/publications/other/Carpenters%20community%20plan%202013%20%28final%29.pdf. Accessed 1 August 2019.
2. Robin Brown of Just Space had a copy of the wiki and Michael Edwards put it on his blog. See Planners Network UK. 2015. 'People's Plans'. https://michaeledwards.org.uk/2015/08/23/planners-network-uk-peoples-plans. Accessed 29 July 2019.
3. Covent Garden Community Association. n.d. 'The CGCA – A Short History'. http://www.covent-garden.org.uk/about/cgca-history. Accessed 29 July 2019.
4. Iain Tuckett. 1988. 'Coin Street: There Is Another Way ...', *Community Development Journal* 23(4): 249–57.

5. Coin Street Community Builders. n.d. 'The Campaign'. http://coinstreet.org/who-we-are/history-background/the-campaign/. Accessed 29 July 2019.

6. London Tenants Federation, Loretta Lees, Just Space and Southwark Notes Archive Group. 2014. *Staying Put: An Anti-Gentrification Handbook for Council Estates in London*. London: Just Space. https://justspacelondon.files.wordpress.com/2014/06/staying-put-web-version-low.pdf. Accessed 1 August 2019

7. Stephanie Butcher, Federica Risi and Alexandre Apsan Frediani, eds. 2019. *University-led Community Partnerships and Social Justice: Exploring Potentials in UCL Bloomsbury and Stratford*. MSc Social Development Practice Student Report in partnership with the Public Engagement Unit of UCL Culture.

8. This point on the relevance of platforms such as WordPress for campaigns was made by the planner and campaigner Marco Picardi during his lecture at the Civic Design UCL Summer School, 2018.

Part III
Next Challenges for Community-Led Regeneration

The Heygate Estate in the London Borough of Southwark was demolished between 2011 and 2014,[1] its residents were displaced[2] and the estate was replaced with a private development. Before demolition, the estate comprised 1194 social rented homes, a total that will decrease to 74 once the scheme is completed. This loss is justified in the developers' viability assessment.[3] In addition, a Transparency International UK report reveals that most of the properties have been sold to foreign investors.[4] Thus the redevelopment of Heygate Estate exemplifies every possible bad practice of estate regeneration.

Sadiq Khan won the London Mayoral Election in May 2016 with a programme prioritising social housing. Since becoming Mayor, he has developed such policy proposals as no net loss of floor space of social rented homes, the like-to-like replacement of tenure in estate regeneration, included in the draft London Plan, and the introduction of a Resident ballot as a pre-condition for GLA funding. Our view is that these policies are still not sufficient. Rather, they are setting conditions for local authorities and developers to demolish social housing. Instead, they should include policies that effectively require local authorities and developers to prioritise refurbishment as opposed to demolition (considering the environmental and social impact that demolition has in comparison to refurbishment),[5] and should be designed for communities to make decisions on their neighbourhoods.[6] However, while these new policies are not yet sufficient, they do make progress in avoiding cases such as the Heygate Estate demolition. Housing campaigns across London have clearly had an impact on policy-making.

The case studies discussed in this book (particularly West Ken Gibbs Green Community Homes (WKGGCH), Cressingham Gardens

Community, Greater Carpenters Neighbourhood Forum and People's Empowerment Alliance for Custom House) demonstrate the considerable progress that communities have made in gaining control over the regeneration of their neighbourhood or strengthening their decision-making power in the period since this research was initiated at the end of 2016. During the coming years, however, they will have to overcome some challenges to make a community-led regeneration of their neighbourhood possible.

On 11 June 2019 we co-organised with Just Space a workshop in Gibbs Green Community Hall to explore these challenges; social housing residents, housing campaigners and scholars involved in activist research were among the participants. Prior to the workshop, discussions among key participants identified four main challenges facing social housing: a) fuel poverty, b) financing of community-led regeneration, c) knowledge exchange between communities, researchers and professionals and d) community organising – including good governance, democratic accountability, reaching the wider community and influencing decision-making. During the workshop, residents from six out of the seven case studies presented in this book and scholars involved in research on social housing regeneration (Loretta Lees, Adam Elliot-Cooper, Joe Penny and the authors of this book) made presentations. The workshop then divided into four discussion groups to focus on the four pre-identified topics. These discussions, summarised below, create the setting for future research into community-led social housing regeneration.

Fuel poverty and residents' control

Of particular importance in resident-led estate regeneration are the interconnected questions of energy provision, estate-wide heating systems and fuel poverty, where the latter is the condition of being unable to afford to keep one's home adequately heated. The unaffordability of energy-related bills is not the only determinant of fuel poverty. Instead, the causes of fuel poverty have to include the lack of maintenance, poor planning and the additional burdens placed on individuals by the failures generated at estate level as these also contribute to this situation.

The mechanisms that cause the problem of fuel poverty are diverse. It remains not so much a passive problem linked to fuel consumption, but rather a general issue relating to the human right to decent habitation. Issues of energy consumption are linked to wider demands concerning accountability over heating services and access to adequate shelter, as well as collective control of its conditions. Homes ought to be fulfilling these human rights obligations – and although people have a right to choose their heating at an individual level, the collective need for a well-maintained and insulated building envelope is also crucial. Individual heating is therefore only good if the building envelope is of good quality – otherwise it leads to fuel poverty due to the need for over-compensation at an individual level.

Attention to maintenance thus has to refer to the building enve-lope as well as to the heating system itself. Many estates across London are faced with heating networks in very poor states of maintenance. Leaseholders are consequently forced to pay for the capital expenditure of renewing collective heating systems, as in the example of Southwark's Gilesmead Estate.[7]

The choices in such situations are problematic, however. For exam-ple, district heating, which is very common among countries in the EU, is less expensive and greener than individual heating systems. However, many examples of such systems across London show that inappropriate choices have been made around procurement and management of con-tracts. Developers typically take short cuts, institute poor management and maintenance arrangements, have weak oversight and low levels of safeguarding for customers and often lock tenants and leaseholders into long-term contracts with monopoly energy providers.[8]

The experience of Myatts Field North in the London Borough of Lambeth is a case in point. Here residents had many issues with the instal-lation of a district heating system and the imposition of an energy monop-oly.[9] This case and the similar experience of residents on Alexandra and Ainsworth Estates, demonstrates the importance of control and account-ability by residents of their own energy provision at estate-level.

While district heating may therefore be better in theory, contracts and procurement can bring difficult challenges for maintenance and management by councils and residents. It can also be problematic for the Registered Social Landlord sector to participate in such projects, as costs may be distributed to residents unfairly.

Alternatively, it is pertinent to consider the feasibility of community-led energy production and the role of the residents. Such systems can include solar panels or other renewables, within a district heating network. However, it is worth bearing in mind the possible points of failure in a dis-trict heating network, which can be both technical and financial. Therefore, examining what projects need to deliver and what are the project's aims is crucial.

The residents' aims could be about greater individual tenant choice or about developing a better large-scale, collective community response. There are also social and governance considerations, inasmuch as such systems involve empowering the residents in matters relating to their own choice of power and energy systems, as well as the control, maintenance and replacement responsibilities for these services. This therefore would include the residents' own individual fuel consumption, but also their collective control over installation, maintenance and refurbishment of the services providing their heating.

Financing community-led regeneration

The case studies presented here, as well as the experience of other estate residents across London, have shown how the demolition of housing can be stopped through the use of some of the planning tools explained here as well as strong and sustained campaigning. Now these successful groups are facing the challenge of leading the regeneration of their neighbourhoods, or of having genuine decision-making power in the regeneration process. When planning for any kind of regeneration (not just community-led), one of the key challenges is how to pay for it. For this reason, we decided to include the topic 'financing community-led regeneration' as one of the discussions in the final workshop. This focused on the available funding schemes and on other sources of funding, such as using the existing resources (land, buildings and potential for solar energy generation) of the neighbourhood.

An important topic that emerged in the discussions was the financial viability of refurbishment vs demolition. Such alternatives need to be appraised, particularly the issue of the cost of refurbishment that would have to be borne by leaseholders. In the case of Cressingham Gardens, the council estimated a very high cost for refurbishment (around £14m–£16m). The residents contested this figure and engaged a quantity surveyor who estimated a cost of £7 million, half of the council's figure. After this the council lowered their estimate to £9.4 million.[10] This situation showed the importance of residents employing their own quantity surveyor as, without such professional inputs, they would have not been able to fight for the refurbishment case.

The remaining part of the discussion focused on sources of funding – in particular, how residents can access funding when giving notice for the Right to Manage[11] and the Right to Transfer,[12] when putting together a People's Plan, and when bringing council decisions to Judicial Review. There is support from central government for communities who wish to apply for the Right to Manage and the Right to Transfer. For the former, it is important to contact the National Federation of Tenant Management Organisations (NFTMO), which can provide support and advice on funding sources, and on recommending lawyers to put together a Tenant Management Organisation (TMO) (or Resident Management Organisation, as Cressingham Gardens residents call it). In the case of Cressingham Gardens, the NFTMO recommended a lawyer to them to set up their Resident Management Organisation; the council paid the lawyer's fees. Once the Right to Manage takes place, the TMO gets an allowance from the local authority to manage repairs and maintenance.

For the People's Plan, Cressingham Gardens used different sources of funding to pay for an architect (a former resident of the estate) and other professional consultants to support them in different parts of the People's Plan. They also used internal expertise, as there were highly qualified residents who dedicated a lot of time and effort to the People's Plan. This includes two chapters dealing with finance. Chapter 7 explains 'Five funding structures and their implication' and explores different options, varying from Lambeth developing the People's Plan to full community ownership, with some options in between that would require partnership between the local authority and the community. Chapter 8 explains different 'Funding sources' and provides a detailed account of different funding options and financial instruments that could be used to fund the People's Plan.[13] The plan also considers other forms of generating income and the possibility of adding more housing. This includes the use of garages for building more homes and the production of energy with solar panels.

For Judicial Reviews, low-income tenants can access legal aid. For further information on this, see chapter 11, 'Using the law and challenging redevelopment through the courts'. Here the funding options are discussed, as are the differences between bringing a council decision to Judicial Review by an individual or by a community.

Finally, another key point derived from the Cressingham Gardens experience was the importance of a productive collaboration between tenants and leaseholders. In particular, because they had different rights, their access to information and to funding could also be different.

Knowledge exchange

Grassroots community groups have usually had years of coping with a range of issues at the local level. A form of embedded knowledge of lived experience has consequently developed which is valuable and needs to be recognised. At the same time, groups have needs for both further skills and spaces for up-skilling people within their groups in order to develop their own solutions to the urban problems they confront. While skills improvement can be offered by external individuals and organisations, such as academic or engaged practitioners, and can include technical subjects, there is also a need for more general information and communications. Making this more widely available would enable groups to be better informed, and to feel involved in the decisions being made in local authorities or at London level, for example.

Underpinning this issue of information and skills improvement for empowerment is the question of power, which has to be shifted. Consultation structures used in the past have repeatedly failed communities, which have become accustomed to failure and being lied to. The sharing of knowledge has to be accompanied by a shift in power relations. As the saying goes: 'Don't do it to me, do it with me'. For example, some places have experienced repeated waves of regeneration investment, starting in the 1980s with Estate Action, Housing Action Trusts, City Action Task Forces and City Challenge and followed, more recently in the 1990s, by the Single Regeneration Budgets (SRB), Estate Renewal Challenge Fund and New Deal for Communities (NDC). The outcomes, in some cases, have been very sparse in terms of local, surviving institutions. Not very much has been left of that investment apart from a sense of long-term failure, disempowerment, lies and acrimony, which has led to embedded civic disenchantment, even trauma.

There is a sense, in some places, that the regeneration programmes had been hijacked, and there remain serious capital investment problems to this day that need to be addressed. These places may be characterised by resident disengagement, linked to lack of trust, which needs to be rebuilt, within and between local groups and other organisations, such as housing associations or the local authority. Thus the displacement that accompanies regeneration can be a displacement both of people and of local institutions and existing social relations.[14]

For any knowledge exchange, engagement or skills improvement process, people must be willing to gather in a room. Yet it can be hard to achieve this. Not only is there the long-term disengagement to deal with, but in some cases a transitory population has also undermined knowledge and engagement. At the same time there may have been area stigmatisation,[15] conflicts and the need to deal with a range of competing priorities.

As a result of the Right to Buy, the diversity of resident tenures increased. More people live now in private rented or housing association properties, and there are also misconceptions about the lived experiences of the different tenured households. All these factors have contributed to a fragmentation of both knowledge and political networks of community organisation.

Disengagement or disenchantment with local political processes are factors that have impacted on knowledge exchanges at a local level. These have been accompanied – and sometimes exacerbated – by cultural differences, especially in areas or estates which are not homogenous in terms of class, incomes, ethnicity or even tenures. These differences must be acknowledged as part of the training and knowledge dissemination as a way to bring people from one estate, or even from different estates, together at a local level. The exchange and empowerment which can lead to greater leadership by community groups can be supported top-down through state interventions, as well as bottom-up. Grassroots communities have solutions to urban problems, in part because of years of campaigning, but they require the tools, spaces and resources to develop these, along with access to the necessary information. However, given that people are being inundated with information, care must be taken with how information is used and the timescales of communication that are set. Often bursts of information come in a short period and then years pass. Alternatively, communities can be drip-fed with information, unrelated to what they themselves need or to their everyday lives.

Housing needs and regeneration pressures are also very urgent. When an individual family or community group needs information and access to knowledge, there is usually a serious time constraint. The people in need of housing do not have the time or skills to familiarise themselves with the complex world of community-led housing; instead they need institutions and resources to share the available information and knowledge. West Ken Gibbs Green Community Homes, as well as People's Empowerment Alliance for Custom House (PEACH), serve here as case studies, illustrating the importance of training communities to collect, utilise and have ownership of their own knowledge.

This can require broad political will, however, to support the building of community infrastructures and resident-led organisations, with resources for community organisers or tenant management workers. Tenant Management Organisations play a part in this ecology of community infrastructures, but these organisations are also complex in terms of governance and management. Other organisations able to play a role can be universities, who can support, through their researchers and students, the building up of community knowledge. This is a political vision of civic agency, based on the capacities of people and communities to solve problems and generate cultures: 'Power in the civic agency model is the "power to" not the "power over"'.[16]

The housing models themselves are flawed and need to be challenged. For example, the salaries paid to housing association chief executives, while they may be in line with other housing professionals, raise serious questions around how they are working and protecting council housing. This, in turn, raises the question of how can social housing be protected. Indeed, one can look beyond TMOs as forms of resident-led governance, recognising that every group is unique though there are commonalities in terms of knowledge support and resourcing. In shaping these challenges to current housing models, greater understanding needs to be shared about 'community-led' options at all levels of local governance. There is also a need to simplify community-led housing funds, processes and support structures. These might seem like utopian models, but there are good examples at grassroots level. At a wider scale, there is a need for more information and knowledge about the bigger picture – what shapes the housing market, the pressures of regeneration, the political decisions and institutions that make up the landscape and shape the dynamics to which residents are subject.

Learning from international experiences is also valuable. The example of Spain is important. Here the social housing conditions are very different to the UK, but there is a strong history of housing movements that are now moving into municipal power and trying to implement new forms of housing. A case in point is the municipal support for new housing policies around the human rights to housing[17] and the new, municipal-led, co-operative housing projects in Barcelona.[18] In Turkey an interesting aspect of the social housing challenge faced by residents attempting to gain more control of regeneration processes is the growing need for legal knowledge and professionals, to counter the increasing closure of democratic arenas for contestation.[19]

Six years ago the London Tenants Federation, Just Space, Southwark Notes Archive Group and Loretta Lees published the pamphlet *Staying Put*, a work that people still use and refer to. These forms of booklet, as information and communication tools, are a way of filtering information; they have a focus on support, disseminating successes as well as hope. The material needs to be presented in a way that is usable and, if in website form, easy to update. Other ways in which these important lived experiences can be shared can include the use of film, oral history recordings, photography and journals. These are all complementary forms, contributing to a community infrastructure of knowledge around housing and regeneration. Our attempt in this book is to build on, and to add to, this work.

Community organising

The fourth topic discussed in the workshop examined the case studies of WKGGCH and PEACH where the importance of community organising to build and motivate strong campaigns, particularly long-lasting ones, needed to be sustained over time. Community organisers are people who dedicate time to bring residents together and help them to establish structures of governance. The workshop discussions focused on four areas: a) how to create a strong campaign, b) how to reach a wider community, c) how to influence decision-making and d) good governance and democratic accountability.

How to create a strong campaign

It is important to have a good point and purpose as the basis for the campaign. This purpose should be *inclusive* and *shared* at the same time: it should include marginalised groups but should also be tailored to different communities. At the same time, the campaign purpose should be shared by the different people who might live within a housing estate. For this reason it is important to establish shared values with clarity and transparency, while keeping in mind the main purpose of the campaign and not lose it. The discussion also focused on the importance of understanding who has decision-making powers and on building relationships with them.

How to reach a wider community

This is one of the key functions of a community organiser. They have to make the campaign as inclusive as possible among all the residents, not just those who engage with activities regularly. In doing so, the language used in the campaign should be accessible to everyone and alienation should be avoided, through meetings, home visiting and continually engaging with people. It is also useful to organise events and activities that can attract a wide diversity of residents, targeting different groups within the neighbourhood and building alliances with close (or not so close) neighbours.

How to influence decision-making

Patience is really important when seeking to influence decision-making. A strong campaign and support from other groups will also assist this end and, similarly to reaching a wider community, it is necessary to identify who the decision-makers are, in order to approach them and interact with them using easily understood language. It is also important to make these decision-makers feel comfortable with the objectives of the campaign (for which appropriate language is again important); a balance of hard contestation and positive engagement often works well. Social media can be a powerful tool to put pressure on local authorities, but it needs to be used very carefully and respectfully. It is important to challenge people in power, but with a non-offensive attitude.

Forms of good governance and democratic accountability

The last area discussed was the balance between informal and formal forms of governance. This is one of the conclusions of this book and a previous publication from this project.[20] As the case studies have shown, the combination of formal and informal forms of governance allows flexibility; at the same time it provides decision-making structures and the necessary organisations to use certain formal tools. The discussion also addressed the importance of codifying rules and behaviour for good communication and relationships within the community. Another proposal was having 'custodians' or good governance in the neighbourhood.

The June workshop closed in a positive and optimistic environment, in which residents had discussed their strategies and achievements so far in proposing community-led regeneration plans. The event demonstrated the potential for residents to share experiences, both with others in a similar situation and with researchers working in collaboration with community groups.

Acknowledgements for Part III

This chapter is very much a collaborative effort emerging from the final sessions of the workshop held in June 2019. We would like to thank Richard Lee, Becky Turner, Elena Besussi, Frances Brill and Jonathan Rosenberg for helping us to plan and facilitate the four discussion topics during the workshop. We would also like to thank Loretta Lees, Adam Elliot-Cooper, Joe Penny, Elizabeth Knowles, who spoke about Alexandra

Road Park Heritage Lottery Fund restoration, and the residents and community organisers who participated in the sessions – including those from WKGG, PEACH, Cressingham Gardens, Greater Carpenters Neighbourhood Forum, Alexandra and Ainsworth Estates, and WECH for their participation on the panel sessions. We would like to thank Just Space for co-organising the workshop with us and WKGGCH for hosting us in their community hall. We would also like to thank all participants for their contribution to the discussion and the workshops.

Notes

1. Southwark Notes. 'Heygate Estate'. https://southwarknotes.wordpress.com/heygate-estate/. Accessed 19 July 2019.
2. London Tenants Federation, Loretta Lees, Just Space and Southwark Notes Archive Group. 2014. *Staying Put: An Anti-Gentrification Handbook for Council Estates in London*. https://justspacelondon.files.wordpress.com/2014/06/staying-put-web-version-low.pdf. Accessed 1 August 2019
3. Oliver Wainwright. 2015. 'Revealed: How Developers Exploit Flawed Planning System to Minimise Affordable Housing', *The Guardian*., 25 June 2015. https://www.theguardian.com/cities/2015/jun/25/london-developers-viability-planning-affordable-social-housing-regeneration-oliver-wainwright. Accessed 10 May 2019.
4. Transparency International UK. 2017. 'Faulty Towers: Understanding the Impact of Overseas Corruption on the London Property Market'. https://www.transparency.org.uk/publications/faulty-towers-understanding-the-impact-of-overseas-corruption-on-the-london-property-market. Accessed 10 May 2019.
5. See a collection of technical evidence on this at UCL Engineering Exchange. 2017. 'Demolition or Refurbishment of Social Housing?' https://www.ucl.ac.uk/engineering-exchange/research-projects/2019/apr/demolition-or-refurbishment-social-housing. Accessed 1 August 2019.
6. See responses from Just Space to the Draft London Plan, the Draft Housing Strategy, the Mayor's Good Practice Guide for Estate Regeneration and the Resident Ballot Requirement Funding Condition at https://justspace.org.uk. Accessed 19 July 2019. See also our own response to the Resident Ballot Requirement Funding Condition at http://communityled.london. Accessed 19 July 2019.
7. Fuel Poverty Action. 2019. *Making Green Come True*. Submission to the Examination in Public of the London Plan, 29 March 2019.
8. Fuel Poverty Action. 2019. *Making Green Come True*. Submission to the Examination in Public of the London Plan, 29 March 2019.
9. Stuart Hodkinson and Chris Essen. 2015. 'Grounding Accumulation by Dispossession in Everyday Life: The Unjust Geographies of Urban Regeneration under the Private Finance Initiative', *International Journal of Law in the Built Environment* 7(1): 81.
10. This was discussed in the event held on 11 June 2019. However, these figures are taken from the interview with two residents that took place on 10 January 2017.
11. Most of the conversation focused on the Right to Manage, as Cressingham Gardens residents had been successful on the Right to Manage.
12. On 11 June 2019 the Secretary of State had not yet arrived at a determination on the Right to Transfer.
13. Cressingham People's Plan. 2016. http://cressinghampeoplesplan.org.uk. Accessed 21 June 2016. Crowdjustice. https://www.crowdjustice.com. Accessed 16 October 2019.
14. See the work of Loretta Lees on multiple types of displacement, in Loretta Lees, Hyun Bang Shin and Ernesto López-Morales, eds. 2015. *Global Gentrifications: Uneven Development and Displacement*. Bristol: Policy Press. Or see Stefano Portelli's 'From the Horizontal to the Vertical: The Displacement of Bon Pastor in Barcelona', *ACME*, forthcoming.

15. On the ideological roots of estate stigmatisation see Ben Campkin's chapter 'Sink Estate Spectacle', in *Remaking London: Decline and Regeneration in Urban Culture*. 2013. London: I. B. Tauris. This is an analysis of the stigmatisation of the Heygate and Aylesbury Estates by publicity-seeking politicians and urbanists.

16. Stephen Hill. 2015. *Reconnecting the Citizen and State through Community Land Trusts and Land Reform in Nine Narratives*. London: The Winston Churchill Memorial Trust. https://www.academia.edu/12082488/Property_Justice_and_Reason_-_Reconnecting_the_Citizen_and_the_State_through_Community_Land_Trusts_and_Land_Reform_April_2015. Accessed 31 July 2019.

17. Barcelona's new *Plan for the Right to Housing 2016–25* includes the building of new social housing resulting through the co-operative sector. See also Ismael Blanco, Yunailis Salazar and Iolanda Bianchi. 2019. 'Urban Governance and Political Change under a Radical Left Government: The Case of Barcelona', *Journal of Urban Affairs* (published online, 2019). https://doi.org/10.1080/07352166.2018.1559648. Accessed 23 January 2020.

18. See the work of Marc Parés, Mara Ferreri and Eduard Cabré, *La coproducció d'habitatge a Catalunya: Orientacions per al món local*, forthcoming, from the COPHAB project in Barcelona on the support by the municipal City government to new co-operatives and co-housing projects. Research under the umbrella of the COPHAB project begun in 2018 on 'Co-production and Participatory Housing Management: Social Initiatives, 2018. Community Capacities and Public Policy Instruments'. 2018. http://commoninghousing.net/projects/cophab. Accessed 31 July 2019.

19. Aylin Topal, Galip L. Yalman and Özlem Çelik. 2019. 'Changing Modalities of Urban Redevelopment and Housing Finance in Turkey: Three Mass Housing Projects in Ankara', *Journal of Urban Affairs* 41(5): 630–53.

20. Pablo Sendra. 2018. 'Assemblages for Community-Led Social Housing Regeneration: Activism, Big Society and Localism', *City* 22 (5–6): 738–62.

Conclusions

After having explored the seven case studies and reviewed the strengths and limitations of the existing planning tools and frameworks for community-led regeneration, we have explained how the available planning tools can be used for opposing demolitions and proposing community-led plans. We have also identified what difficulties and limitations residents might find, and how these limitations can be overcome.

Planning frameworks such as neighbourhood planning have certain limitations on opposing local authorities' plans. This is because neighbourhood forums and areas need to be designated by the planning authority, and the Neighbourhood Plan needs to comply with other policy documents issued by the same local authority. Such frameworks also require time commitment, as the process from designation of the neighbourhood forum until the plan is brought into force is long. There are also questions on the implementation of the plan and the funding for implementing it.

From the case studies presented here, only one has submitted a Neighbourhood Plan. This occurred in a very particular condition, where the planning authority (London Legacy Development Corporation) was different from the borough (London Borough of Newham). Other tools, such as the Right to Transfer, have not been fully tested, since none of the cases where this legislation has been used have yet been completed. Two of the case studies presented here have given notice for the Right to Transfer, but only one of them, Cressingham Gardens, has been successful in being approved by the Secretary of State. This determination happened while this book was being written, so it is not yet possible to analyse how the transfer has taken place. Despite not being fully tested, the Right to Transfer, if and when confirmed by a Resident ballot, could save Cressingham Gardens from demolition and give residents control over the regeneration of their neighbourhood.

Despite these limitations, the case studies have thus demonstrated that the combination of these formal strategies with other forms of informal planning, activism and campaigning is very effective in opposing demolition and proposing alternative plans. Some of them have combined formal planning and legal tools with developing a non-statutory People's Plan that has brought together a residents' vision for the neighbourhood. The People's Plan, in combination with other strategies, has proved to be a very effective strategy. Its effectiveness lies in the flexibility it provides, and in the way that it can be put together in a relatively short time. In the case of Greater Carpenters Neighbourhood Forum, putting together a community plan (equivalent to a People's Plan) provided an opportunity for residents to put together a community vision; it served as a first step before committing to the neighbourhood planning route. From this case study, we conclude that putting together a community plan or a People's Plan can be a good first step for making the decision on whether neighbourhood planning is a good option or not. In the case of Cressingham Gardens Community, the People's Plan contributed to their success in getting approval by the Secretary of State for continuing with their Right to Transfer.

Since we started this project at the end of 2016, the situation of these housing estates and their residents has changed. In many cases, after years of campaigning, residents are succeeding in stopping the demolition of their homes and gaining a stronger say in their neighbourhood's future. In all cases the campaigns are still ongoing, and therefore it is not clear whether they will manage to achieve a community-led regeneration, but this remains a possibility for all the campaigns. Some of the campaigns examined in this report have already managed to complete a community-led regeneration. One such is the case of Walterton and Elgin Community Homes (WECH), which completed the transfer of housing from the local authority to a community-owned housing association in the early 1990s, and is now building new social housing on the rooftops of some of their blocks. Alexandra and Ainsworth Estates residents managed to get funding and to work in partnership with their local authority in refurbishing their park. Cressingham Gardens Community have succeeded in getting approval for both the Right to Manage and the Right to Transfer.

From the analysis of the case studies and the tools and strategies, we can divide the specific conclusions into the following three sections.

A toolkit for different steps of the 'ladder of participation'

The tools that we have explained in this report provide different possibilities for communities participating in the decision-making process around the regeneration of their neighbourhoods.[1] In her seminal paper 'A Ladder of Citizen Participation', Sherry Arnstein defined a ladder with eight degrees of participation (fig.C.1), with 'manipulation' at the bottom and 'citizen control' at the top.[2]

Figure C.1 Cartoon by Rob Cowan from *Built Environment* 45, nos 1 and 2, 2019. © Alexandrine Press.

In many of the case studies explained here, the discontent felt by residents towards the council's approach to regeneration and/or the threat of seeing their homes demolished has led residents to seek control of the regeneration process of their homes. This happens particularly when the council does not listen to the residents and wants to continue with demolition. In those cases, residents seek control of their estate to prevent the demolition of their homes. This has resulted in campaigns aspiring to be at the very top of the ladder and using strategies such as giving notice for a Right to Transfer (as West Kensington and Gibbs Green or Cressingham Gardens residents have done).

However, citizens' control is not the only option to have a meaningful participation. Depending on each situation, and on the residents' intentions, other steps of the ladder can also work. The top three steps of the ladder, named by Arnstein as 'degrees of citizen power', should be the aspiration of every social housing regeneration scheme. These three steps are 'citizen control', 'delegated power' and 'partnership'. Many of the tools explained here can lead to these three levels of participation.

In any case, the minimum requirement for any regeneration scheme, in case the community is not willing to take a leading role, must be to run a lawful consultation (step 4 of the ladder). In England and Wales, the Principles of Fair Consultation, explained in chapter 11 of this book, set out very clearly what a lawful consultation must be. Residents must be given sufficient time and information to participate, and their responses to the consultations have to be heard and considered in the scheme (among other requirements). Any consultation that does not meet these principles can be challenged through a Judicial Review.

However, there are some consultation processes that, despite legally meeting the Principles of Fair Consultation, still produce discontent among residents and campaigners. The reason for this is because local authorities hold the power to run these consultation processes, and they can formulate the questions to get the responses they want. When this happens, the consultation is closer to the 'manipulation' step of the ladder.

Building capacity for community-led regeneration

The book has explored how the combination of strategies, the interaction between communities, the creation of networks and the access to support can make campaigns stronger in resisting demolition and proposing alternatives. The book has identified three particular situations, combination of facts, strategies and alliances that make campaigns stronger in resisting demolition.[3]

First, communities using a combination of formal organisations, such as neighbourhood forums or Community Land Trusts, along with informal organisation and campaigns, have a strong capacity to resist demolition and propose alternative plans, since they have the ability to engage both in formal planning strategies (within existing planning frameworks) and in informal strategies (such as demonstrating or occupying).

The combination of these formal planning tools and informal strategies is the most effective way to resist demolition and propose alternative plans. Second, the creation of networks and the exchange of knowledge between campaigns going through similar situations can strengthen their campaigns. Resident groups learn from each other. When communities are successful using a particular strategy, this serves as precedent for other groups. Third, as some of the case studies have shown, the access to support from professionals (such as community organisers, planners, architects, lawyers and surveyors) and from researchers (through collaboration with universities) can strengthen campaigns and also build local knowledge of planning within the community.

What is the impact of campaigning?

The research demonstrates that campaigning does have an impact. In those case studies fighting against demolition, the work has either been stopped or delayed. In addition to that, some of the case studies presented here, such as WECH or Alexandra and Ainsworth Estates, have managed then to lead, or to have an important role in, the regeneration of their neighbourhoods.

Housing activism implies long-lasting campaigns, which can be very tiring and energy-consuming for residents. The presence of community organisers and housing organisers, such as in the cases of People's Empowerment Alliance for Custom House (PEACH) or West Ken Gibbs Green Community Homes, is thus very important in keeping residents motivated and supported. Cases such as PEACH, which invested a large proportion of its Big Local funding into community organising, demonstrate the importance of community organising in bringing a community vision together, and in getting communities to have an important role in decision-making.

We would like to finish this book with a message of hope and optimism for campaigners. Since we started this research, some of the campaigns we have studied have made considerable achievements in their campaigns. While they are still in the process of achieving what Arnstein would define as 'degrees of citizen power', they are getting closer. Housing campaigners are starting to influence decision-making at a neighbourhood scale, at a local authority scale and, in the case of London, at a metropolitan scale through the consultation process on the Mayor of London's policy documents (see chapter 10).[4] The achievements of these campaigns can motivate other activist groups to resist and fight for their rights, as well as provide for knowledge transfer between individual campaigns. In addition to this, the rise of activism, the increasing politicisation of estate resident communities, along with other housing groups and the prominent denouncing of situations of injustice, can play an important role in influencing, reversing or indeed finding alternative policies to the politics of austerity.

Notes

1. Sherry R. Arnstein. 1969. 'A Ladder of Citizen Participation', *Journal of the American Planning Association* 35(4): 210–24.
2. Sherry R. Arnstein. 1969. 'A Ladder of Citizen Participation', *Journal of the American Planning Association* 35(4): 210–24.
3. Pablo Sendra, 2018. 'Assemblages for Community-Led Social Housing Regeneration: Activism, Big Society and Localism', *City* 22 (5–6): 738–62.
4. Pablo Sendra and Daniel Fitzpatrick. 2020. 'Time to Be an Activist: Recent Successes in London Housing Activism', in Susannah Bunce, Nicola Livingstone, Susan Moore and Alan Walks, eds., *Critical Dialogues of Urban Governance, Development and Activism, London and Toronto*. London: UCL Press.

Bibliography

Alexandra and Ainsworth Estates Tenants and Residents Association. http://alexandraandainsworth. org. Accessed 31 July 2019.

Alexandra and Ainsworth Estates Tenants and Residents Association / Lefkos Kyriacou (resident and architect). n.d. 'A Short History of the Alexandra and Ainsworth Estate'. http://alexandraandainsworth.org/estate-history-3. Accessed 26 July 2019.

Ajuntamiento de Barcelona. 2016. Barcelona Right to Housing Plan 2016–2025. https://habitatge. barcelona/en/strategy/right-to-housing-plan. Accessed 23 January 2020;

Ambrose, Peter and Stone, Julia. 2010. *Happiness, Heaven and Hell in Paddington: A Comparative Study of the Empowering Management Practices of WECH*. Brighton: University of Sussex.

Anson, Brian. 1981. *I'll Fight You for It: Behind the Struggle for Covent Garden, 1966–74*. London: Jonathan Cape.

Architects for Social Housing. https://architectsforsocialhousing.co.uk. Accessed 30 July 2019.

Architects for Social Housing. 2016. 'Feasibility Study Report: West Kensington and Gibbs Green Estates. New Homes and Improvements without Demolition'. https://architectsforsocialhousing. files.wordpress.com/2016/08/wkgg_report_rev3.pdf. Accessed 23 July 2019.

Arnstein, Sherry Phyllis. 1969. 'A Ladder of Citizen Participation', *Journal of the American Planning Association* 35(4): 216–24.

Barcelona Right to Housing Plan for 2016–2025. 2017 Assessment. http://habitatge.barcelona/ sites/default/files/pla_del_dret_a_lhabitatge_de_barcelona_2016-2025-en-gb.pdf. Accessed 23 January 2020.

Barker, Nathaniel. 2019. 'Council Could Issue Order to Take Earl's Court Site from Developer, Claims Khan', *Inside Housing* (19 July 2019) https://www.insidehousing.co.uk/news/news/council-could-issue-order-to-take-earls-court-site-from-developer-claims-khan-62364. Accessed 29 July 2019.

Bar Pro Bono Unit/Advocate. https://weareadvocate.org.uk/. Accessed 16 October 2019.

Barratt, Luke. 2019. 'Council Demands Return of Earls Court Estates', *Inside Housing*, 18 January 2018). https://www.insidehousing.co.uk/news/news/council-demands-return-of-earls-court-estates-54087. Accessed 23 July 2019.

Besussi, Elena. 2018. 'Localism and Neighbourhood Planning', in J. Ferm and J. Tomaney, eds., *Planning Practice. Critical Perspectives from the UK*. Routledge: London.

Billings, Henrietta. 2015. 'Building of the Month', *Twentieth Century Society* (August 2015). https:// c20society.org.uk/botm/cressingham-gardens-lambeth/. Accessed 15 October 2019.

Blanco, Ismael, Salazar, Yunailis and Bianchi, Iolanda. 2019. 'Urban Governance and Political Change under a Radical Left Government: The Case of Barcelona', *Journal of Urban Affairs* (published online, 2019). https://doi.org/10.1080/07352166.2018.1559648. Accessed 23 January 2020.

Brown, Gavin. 2014. 'Objecting to Apartheid: Building a Non-Stop Protest in 1980s' London', *V&A Blog* (16 May 2014). https://www.vam.ac.uk/blog/disobedient-objects/objecting-apartheid-building-non-stop-protest-1980s-london. Accessed 30 July 2019.

Butcher, Stephanie, Risi, Federica and Frediani, Alexandre A., eds. 2019. *University-led Community Partnerships and Social Justice: Exploring Potentials in UCL Bloomsbury and Stratford*. MSc Social Development Practice Student Report in partnership with the Public Engagement Unit of UCL Culture (May 2019).

Cameron, Amanda. 2018. 'Victory for Foxhill Residents as Judge Quashes Approval of Curo's Plans for Demolition – Live Updates'. *SomersetLive* (20 June 2018). https://www.somersetlive. co.uk/in-your-area/victory-foxhill-residents-after-judge-1695031. Accessed 16 October 2019.

Campkin, Ben. 2013. 'Sink Estate Spectacle', in *Remaking London: Decline and Regeneration in Urban Culture*. London: I. B. Tauris.

Capital & Counties Properties PLC. 'Annual Report & Accounts 2015'. http://www.annualreports.com/HostedData/AnnualReportArchive/C/LSE_CAPC_2015.pdf. Accessed 29 July 2019.

Change.org. 2016. 'Votes for Residents on Estates Facing Regeneration'. https://www.change.org/p/sadiq-khan-votes-for-residents-on-estates-facing-regeneration-e38816c6-4a5f-4405-b9b4-bedd946eb9f6. Accessed 1 August 2019.

City Life / Vida Urbana. http://www.clvu.org. Accessed 1 August 2019.

Civil Exchange. 2015. *Whose Society? The Final Big Society Audit*. http://www.civilexchange.org.uk/wp-content/uploads/2015/01/Whose-Society_The-Final-Big-Society-Audit_final.pdf. Accessed 3 March 2017.

Civil Procedure Rule, Part 45: Fixed Costs. https://www.justice.gov.uk/courts/procedure-rules/civil/rules/part45-fixed-costs. Accessed 16 October 2019.

Civil Procedure Rules, Part 54: Judicial Review and Statutory Review. https://www.justice.gov.uk/courts/procedure-rules/civil/rules/part54. Accessed 16 October 2019.

Coin Street Community Builders. n.d. 'The Campaign'. https://coinstreet.org/about-us/history-background/the-campaign/. Accessed 29 July 2019.

Colomb, Claire. 2017. 'Participation and Conflict in the Formation of Neighbourhood Areas and Forums in "Super-Diverse" Cities', in Sue Brownill and Quintin Bradley, eds., *Localism and Neighbourhood Planning*. Policy Press: Bristol;

Community-Led Housing London. https://www.communityledhousing.london. Accessed 1 August 2019.

COPHAB. 'Co-production and Participatory Housing Management: Social Initiatives, Community Capacities and Public Policy Instruments'. 2018. http://commoninghousing.net/projects/cophab. Accessed 31 July 2019.

Covent Garden Community Association. n.d. 'The CGCA – A Short History'. http://www.covent-garden.org.uk/about/cgca-history. Accessed 29 July 2019.

Cressingham People's Plan. 2016. http://cressinghampeoplesplan.org.uk. Accessed 21 June 2016.

Crowdjustice. https://www.crowdjustice.com. Accessed 16 October 2019.

Department for Communities and Local Government. October 2012. 'Community Right to Bid: Non-Statutory Advice Note for Local Authorities'. https://assets.publishing.service.gov.uk/government/uploads/system/uploads/attachment_data/file/14880/Community_Right_to_Bid_-_Non-statutory_advice_note_for_local_authorities.pdf. Accessed 1 August 2019.

Department for Communities and Local Government. 2014. 'Community Infrastructure'. https://www.gov.uk/guidance/community-infrastructure-levy. Accessed 31 May 2017.

Environmental Law Foundation. https://elflaw.org. Accessed 16 October 2019.

Equality Act 2010, Section 149: Public Sector Equality Duty. http://www.legislation.gov.uk/ukpga/2010/15/section/149. Accessed 16 October 2019.

Focus E15 Campaign. '10 Things to Learn from Focus E15 campaign'. https://focuse15.org/2018/09/30/10-things-to-learn-from-focus-e15-campaign. Accessed 30 July 2019.

Focus E15 Campaign. 2015. 'About Us'. https://focuse15.org/about. Accessed 6 June 2017.

Focus E15 Campaign. 2015. 'E15 Open House Occupation'. https://focuse15.org/e15-open-house-occupation. Accessed 6 June 2017.

Focus E15 Campaign. 2019. 'Legal Complaint Served – This Could Go to the High Court Say Public Interest Law Centre' 23 July 2019). https://focuse15.org/2019/07/23/legal-complaint-served-this-could-go-to-the-high-court-says-public-interest-law-centre. Accessed 30 July 2019.

Focus E15 Campaign. 2019. 'Newham Residents' Complaint to Mayor at Full Council Meeting' (16 July 2019). https://focuse15.org/2019/07/16/newham-residents-complaint-to-mayor-at-full-council-meeting. Accessed 30 July 2019.

Focus E15 Campaign. 2015. 'Sylvia's Corner'. https://focuse15.org/sylvias-corner/. Accessed 6 June 2017.

Frediani, Alexandre, Butcher, Stephanie and Watt, Paul, eds. 2013. *Regeneration and Well-Being in East London: Stories from Carpenters Estate*. London: The Bartlett Development Planning Unit, UCL. https://issuu.com/dpu-ucl/docs/carpenters-estate-london. Accessed 23 January 2020.

Friends of Alexandra Road Park. https://friendsofalexandraroadpark.com. Accessed 26 July 2019. Website no longer available.

Friends of Alexandra Park. 'Restoring the Park'. https://friendsofalexandraroadpark.com/about/restoring-the-park/. Accessed 26 July 2019. Website no longer available.

Fuel Poverty Action. 2019. *Making Green Come True*. Submission to the Examination in Public of the London Plan (29 March 2019).

Grayston, Rose. 2017. *Slipping Through the Loophole: How Viability Assessments are Reducing Affordable Housing Supply in England*. London: Shelter.

Greater Carpenters Neighbourhood Forum. 2013. 'Carpenters Community Plan 2013'. http://www.londontenants.org/publications/other/Carpenters%20community%20plan%20 2013%20%28final%29.pdf. Accessed 1 August 2019.

Greater Carpenters Neighbourhood Forum. 2016. 'Achievements. https://greater-carpenters. co.uk/our-work/achievements/. Accessed 4 December 2017.

Greater Carpenters Neighbourhood Forum. 2016. 'Assets of Community Value'. https://greater-carpenters.co.uk/our-work/achievements/assets-of-community-value/. Accessed 17 July 2017.

Greater Carpenters Neighbourhood Forum. 2017. 'Greater Carpenters Neighbourhood Plan. 4th Draft 6th February 2017'. https://greater-carpenters.co.uk/our-work/greater-carpenters-neighbourhood-plan/. Accessed 23 January 2020.

Greater Carpenters Neighbourhood Forum. 2017. 'Pre-submission Neighbourhood Plan and Evidence-Based Documents'. https://greater-carpenters.co.uk/2017/10/29/consultation-draft-stage-2017/. Accessed 17 July 2019.

Greater Carpenters Neighbourhood Forum. 2019. 'Greater Carpenters Neighbourhood Plan 2019–2028. Submission Version May 2019', p. 20. https://greater-carpenters.co.uk/our-work/greater-carpenters-neighbourhood-plan/. Accessed 23 January 2020.

Greater London Authority. 2019. 'GLA Capital Funding Guide: Section 8: Resident Ballots for Estate Regeneration Projects'. https://www.london.gov.uk/sites/default/files/15_section_8._resident_ballots_clean_feb_2019–2.pdf. Accessed 1 August 2019.

Hartmann, Chester, Keating, Dennis and LeGates, Richard, with Turner, Steve. 1982. *Displacement: How to Fight It*. San Francisco: National Housing Law Project.

Hill, Stephen. 2015. *Reconnecting the Citizen and State through Community Land Trusts and Land Reform in Nine Narratives*. London: The Winston Churchill Memorial Trust. https://www.academia.edu/12082488/Property_Justice_and_Reason_-_Reconnecting_the_Citizen_and_the_State_through_Community_Land_Trusts_and_Land_Reform_April_2015. Accessed 31 July 2019.

Historic England. 2019. 'How To Get Historic Buildings or Sites Protected Through Listing'. https://historicengland.org.uk/listing/apply-for-listing/. Accessed 28 July 2019.

Historic England. 2019. 'Listed Buildings'. https://historicengland.org.uk/listing/what-is-designation/listed-buildings/. Accessed 26 July 2019.

Historic England. 2019. 'Living in a Grade I, Grade II* or Grade II Listed Building'. https://historicengland.org.uk/advice/your-home/owning-historic-property/listed-building/. Accessed 26 July 2019.

Hodkinson, Stuart. 2019. *Safe as Houses: Private Greed, Political Negligence and Housing Policy After Grenfell*. Manchester: Manchester University Press.

Hodkinson, Stuart and Essen, Chris. 2015. 'Grounding Accumulation by Dispossession in Everyday Life: The Unjust Geographies of Urban Regeneration under the Private Finance Initiative', *International Journal of Law in the Built Environment* 7(1): 72–91.

Hopkirk, Elizabeth. 2019. 'Camden Brings in Levitt Bernstein to Protect Alexandra Road', *Building Design* (26 July 2019). https://www.bdonline.co.uk/news/camden-brings-in-levitt-bernstein-to-protect-alexandra-road/5100804.article#.XTq_9ORF6pc.twitter. Accessed 27 July 2019.

Hopkirk, Elizabeth. 2019. 'Council Works "Vandalising" Neave Brown's Masterpiece', *Building Design* (12 July 2019). https://www.bdonline.co.uk/news/council-works-vandalising-neave-browns-masterpiece/5100578.article. Accessed 27 July 2019.

'Housing Act 1985: Management Agreements with Tenant Management Organisations'. https://www.legislation.gov.uk/ukpga/1985/68/section/27AB. Accessed 27 July 2019.

Just Space. 2015. *London For All! A Handbook for Community and Small Business Groups Fighting to Retain Workspace for London's Diverse Economies*. London: Just Space and New Economics Foundation.

Just Space. 2016. 'Towards a Community-Led Plan for London Policy Directions and Proposals'. https://justspace.org.uk/the-community-led-alternative-plan. Accessed 1 August 2019.

Just Space. 2017. 'Collective Feedback from Round Table Discussion of the GLA's Recent Draft Good Practice Guide to Estate Regeneration'. https://justspacelondon.files.wordpress.com/2017/03/professor-loretta-lees-gla-draft-guidance-council-estates-feedback.pdf. Accessed 1 August 2019.

Just Space. 2017. 'Draft Good Practice Guide to Estate Regeneration – Mayor of London: Response by Just Space'. https://justspacelondon.files.wordpress.com/2017/03/js-response-on-estate-regeneration-march-2017.pdf. Accessed 1 August 2019.

Just Space. 2017. 'Estate Regeneration: Start Again'. https://justspace.org.uk/2017/03/14/estate-regeneration-start-again/. Accessed 30 November 2019.

Just Space. 2017. 'Housing: Not Good Enough'. https://justspace.org.uk/2017/12/07/housing-not-good-enough. Accessed 31 July 2019.

Just Space. 2018. 'Estate Ballots'. https://justspace.org.uk/2018/04/13/estate-ballots/. Accessed 31 July 2019.

Just Space. 'About Just Space'. https://justspace.org.uk/about/. Accessed 31 July 2019.

Just Space. 2019. 'Actual Equalities Study at Last'. https://justspace.org.uk/2019/04/28/actual-equalities-study-at-last. Accessed 1 August 2019.

Just Space. 2019. 'Grave Weaknesses in the London Plan'. 2019. https://justspace.org.uk/2019/02/26/grave-weaknesses-in-the-london-plan. Accessed 1 August 2019.

Just Space. 2019. 'Inspectors Taking Equality Seriously'. https://justspace.org.uk/2019/03/13/inspectors-taking-equality-seriously. Accessed 1 August 2019.

Leathermarket JMB. 'Who are Leathermarket JMB?'. http://www.leathermarketjmb.org.uk/about-jmb/. Accessed 1 August 2019.

Lees, Loretta, Shin, Hyun Bang and López-Morales, Ernesto, eds. 2015. *Global Gentrifications: Uneven Development and Displacement*. Bristol: Policy Press.

Localism Act 2011. http://www.legislation.gov.uk/ukpga/2011/20/contents/enacted. Accessed 1 August 2019.

Locality. 2016. 'About'. http://locality.org.uk/about/. Accessed 21 February 2017.

Locality. 2016. 'Neighbourhood Plans Roadmap Guide'. An updated version of this guide can be found on https://neighbourhoodplanning.org/wp-content/uploads/NP_Roadmap_online_full.pdf. Accessed 31 July 2019.

London Borough of Hammersmith and Fulham. 2013. 'Conditional Land Sale Agreement in Respect of the Land of West Kensington and Gibbs Green Estates'. https://www.lbhf.gov.uk/sites/default/files/section_attachments/clsa_-_main_body.pdf. Accessed 23 July 2019.

London Borough of Newham. 2017. 'Carpenters Estate Newsletter Update – March 2017'. https://www.newham.gov.uk/Documents/Business/CarpentersEstateNewsletterUpdateMarch2017.pdf. Accessed 23 January 2020.

London Legacy Development Corporation. 2014. 'Local Plan 2015 to 20'. https://www.queenelizabetholympicpark.co.uk/planning-authority/planning-policy/neighbourhood-planning. Accessed 23 January 2020.pdf. Accessed 17 July 2019.

London Legacy Development Corporation. 2019. 'Neighbourhood Planning'. https://www.queenelizabetholympicpark.co.uk/planning-authority/planning-policy/neighbourhood-planning. Accessed 23 January 2020.

London Legacy Development Corporation. 2015. 'Site Allocation SA3.4 – Greater Carpenters District'. http://www.queenelizabetholympicpark.co.uk/-/media/lldc/local-plan/31-march/site-allocation-sa34-response-to-inspector-31st-march-2015.ashx?la=en. Accessed 23 January 2020. Accessed 23 January 2020.

London Tenants Federation, Lees, Loretta, Just Space and Southwark Notes Archive Group. 2014. *Staying Put: An Anti-Gentrification Handbook for Council Estates in London*. London: Just Space. https://justspacelondon.files.wordpress.com/2014/06/staying-put-web-version-low.pdf. Accessed 1 August 2019.

Mayor of London. 2018. *Better Homes for Local People – The Mayor's Good Practice Guide to Estate Regeneration*. London: Greater London Authority. https://www.london.gov.uk/what-we-do/housing-and-land/improving-quality/estate-regeneration. Accessed 23 January 2020.

Mayor of London. 2018. *London Housing Strategy*. London: Greater London Authority. https://www.london.gov.uk/sites/default/files/2018_lhs_london_housing_strategy.pdf. Accessed 29 November 2019.

Mayor of London. 2018. 'The Mayor's Draft Good Practice Guide to Estate Regeneration: Consultation Summary Report'. https://www.london.gov.uk/sites/default/files/draft-good-practice-guide-to-estate-regeneration-main-consultation-summary-report.pdf. Accessed 30 November 2019.

Mayor of London. 2019. 'Draft London Plan – Consolidated Suggested Changes Version July 2019'. https://www.london.gov.uk/what-we-do/planning/london-plan/new-london-plan/draft-london-plan-consolidated-suggested-changes-version-july-2019. Accessed 1 August 2019.

Mayor of London. 2019. 'London Community Housing Fund' (January 2019). https://www.london.gov.uk/sites/default/files/london_chf_prospectus_0.pdf. Accessed 1 August 2019.

Mayor of London, London Assembly. 2018. 'Estate Regeneration'. https://www.london.gov.uk/what-we-do/housing-and-land/improving-quality/estate-regeneration. Accessed 1 August 2019.

Mayor of London, London Assembly. 2018. 'FOI – Estate Regeneration Schemes in London' (March 2018). https://www.london.gov.uk/about-us/governance-and-spending/sharing-our-information/

freedom-information/foi-disclosure-log/foi-estate-regeneration-schemes-london. Accessed 16 July 2019.

Mayor of London, London Assembly. 2018. 'Tackling London's Housing Crisis'. https://www.london. gov.uk/what-we-do/housing-and-land/tackling-londons-housing-crisis. Accessed 1 August 2019.

Mayor of London, London Assembly. 2019. 'Inspector's Report'. https://www.london.gov.uk/what-we-do/planning/london-plan/new-london-plan/inspectors-report. Accessed 29 November 2019.

Ministry of Housing, Communities and Local Government. 2014. 'Guidance: Neighbourhood Planning'. Published 6 March 2014; last updated 9 May 2019. https://www.gov.uk/guidance/neighbourhood-planning-2. Accessed 1 August 2019.

Ministry of Housing, Communities and Local Government. 'Housing (Right to Transfer from a Local Authority Landlord) (England) Regulations 2013'. https://www.gov.uk/government/uploads/system/uploads/attachment_data/file/256523/The_Housing__Right_To_Transfer_from_A_Local_Authority_Landlord___England__Regulations_2013.pdf. Accessed 27 July 2019.

Ministry of Housing, Communities and Local Government. 2019. 'Right to Transfer Determinations: West Kensington and Gibbs Green Estates'. 9 July 2019. https://assets.publishing.service.gov.uk/government/uploads/system/uploads/attachment_data/file/816103/West_Ken_Gibbs_Green_determination_letter_Redacted.pdf. Accessed 16 July 2019.

Ministry of Housing, Communities and Local Government. 2019. 'Right to Transfer determinations: Cressingham Gardens Estate'. 9 July 2019. https://assets.publishing.service.gov.uk/government/uploads/system/uploads/attachment_data/file/816102/Cressingham_Gardens_determination_letter_Redacted.pdf. Accessed 16 July 2019.

Minton, Anna. 2018. 'The Price of Regeneration', *Places Journal*. https://placesjournal.org/article/the-price-of-regeneration-in-london. Accessed 18 November 2019.

Morris, Aggie, Devenyns, Alice, Colombo, Cecilia, Vila, Dolors, Cort, Dominic, Loizou, Iacovos, Manzini Ceinar, Irene, Barson, Leslie, Wyss, Ursula, Sendra Pablo. 2019. *Towards a Co-Design Process: An Alternative to Demolition for William Dunbar and William Saville Tower Blocks, South Kilburn*. London: Civic Design CPD Course. The Bartlett School of Planning, UCL.

My Community, Locality. https://mycommunity.org.uk. Accessed 31 July 2019.

My Community, Locality. 'Assets of Community Value & Right to Bid'. https://mycommunity.org.uk/take-action/land-and-building-assets/assets-of-community-value-right-to-bid/. Accessed 31 July 2019.

My Community, Locality; The Social Investment Business; Local Government Regulation. 2016. 'Community Right to Bid: Understanding the Community Right to Bid'. https://mycommunity.org.uk/wp-content/uploads/2016/09/Understanding-the-Community-Right-to-Bid.pdf. Accessed 1 August 2019.

Natarajan, Lucy. 2019. 'Outlooks on Participating', *Built Environment* 45(1).

National Federation of Tenant Management Organisations. 'Toolbox of the National Federation of Tenant Management Organisations'. http://www.nftmo.co.uk/content/content_toolbox.html. Accessed 27 July 2019.

National Federation of Tenant Management Organisations. 2012. 'Streamlined Common Assessment Model Standards 2012'. http://www.nftmo.co.uk/numo_img/library/Streamlined_CAM_Standards_2012.pdf. Accessed 27 July 2019.

Neighbourhood Planners. London. 2016. Neighbourhood Element of the Community Infrastructure Levy (CIL): The London Experience. https://140d5992-3079-4eb8-bf8d-7a7c1aa9d1df.filesusr.com/ugd/95f6a3_684e0bae1dec48c9a7edd92f485a0bee.pdf. Accessed 26 November 2019

Neighbourhood Planners London. 2017. 'London's Local Plans: Are They Supporting Neighbourhood Planning?' http://docs.wixstatic.com/ugd/95f6a3_6d2d4b5b624c44fd963fedcea470d28d.pdf. Accessed 31 July 2019.

Neighbourhood Planning, Locality. 2018. 'Neighbourhood Development Orders (Including Community Right to Build Orders)'. https://neighbourhoodplanning.org/toolkits-and-guidance/neighbourhood-development-orders-community-right-build-orders/. Accessed 1 August 2019.

New London Architecture. 2019. 'New London Awards 2019 Winners'. https://www.newlondonarchitecture.org/whats-on/new-london-awards/new-london-awards/new-london-awards-2019-winners. Accessed 1 August 2019.

Newton, Rachel and Tunstall, Rebecca. 2012. *Lessons for Localism: Tenant Self-Management*. London: Urban Forum. See Anne Power and Rebecca Tunstall. 1995. Swimming Against the Tide: Polarisation or Progress on 20 Unpopular Council Estates, 1980–1995. Joseph Rowntree Foundation: York.

Parés, Marc, Ferreri, Mara and Cabré, Eduard. Forthcoming. *La coproducció d'habitatge a Catalunya: Orientacions per al món local*. Barcelona: COPHAB.

Parker, Gavin, Lynn, Tessa and Wargent, Matthew. 2014. 'User Experience of Neighbourhood Planning in England. London'. Report. London: Locality. http://mycommunity.org.uk/wp-content/uploads/2016/08/User-experience-executive-study.pdf. Accessed 31 May 2017.

Planning Advisory Group. 1965. *The Future of Development Plans*. HMSO: London.

Planning and Compulsory Purchase Act 2004, Section 19: Preparation of Local Development Documents. http://www.legislation.gov.uk/ukpga/2004/5/section/19. Accessed 26 October 2019.

Planners Network UK. 2015. 'People's Plans'. https://michaeledwards.org.uk/2015/08/23/planners-network-uk-peoples-plans. Accessed 29 July 2019.

'People's Plans'. https://michaeledwards.org.uk/2015/08/23/planners-network-uk-peoples-plans. Accessed 29 July 2019.

Portelli, Stefano. Forthcoming. 'From the Horizontal to the Vertical: The Displacement of Bon Pastor in Barcelona', *ACME*.

Porter, Libby. 2009. *Unlearning the Colonial Cultures of Planning*. Farnham: Ashgate.

Power, Anne and Tunstall, Rebecca. 1995. *Swimming Against the Tide: Polarisation or Progress on 20 Unpopular Council Estates*, 1980–1995. Joseph Rowntree Foundation: York.

Public Works Studio. 'About Us'. https://publicworksstudio.com/en/about. Accessed 1 August 2019.

Public Law Project. 2019. 'An Introduction to Judicial Review' (6 February 2019). https://publiclawproject.org.uk/resources/an-introduction-to-judicial-review-2/. Accessed 16 October 2019.

R (Bokrosova) v London Borough of Lambeth [2015] EWHC 3386 (Admin). http://www.bailii.org/ew/cases/EWHC/Admin/2015/3386.html. Accessed 23 January 2020.

R (Buckley) v Bath and North East Somerset Council & Anor [2018] EWHC 1551 (Admin) (20 June 2018). http://www.bailii.org/ew/cases/EWHC/Admin/2018/1551.html. Accessed 16 October 2019.

R (Moseley) v London Borough of Haringey [2014] UKSC 56 (29 October 2014). http://www.bailii.org/uk/cases/UKSC/2014/56.html. Accessed 26 October 2019.

R (Plant) v Lambeth LBC [2017] PTSR 453. http://www.bailii.org/ew/cases/EWHC/Admin/2016/3324.html. Accessed 27 January 2020.

R v Brent London Borough Council, ex. p. Gunning [1985] 84 LGR 168.

Repensar Bonpastor. https://repensarbonpastor.wordpress.com. Accessed 1 August 2019.

Right to the City Alliance. 2010. 'We Call These Projects Home'. Report. Right to the City Alliance. https://righttothecity.org/cause/we-call-these-projects-home. Accessed 1 August 2019.

Rosenberg, Jonathan. 2011. *Measuring the Benefits of Empowerment through Community Ownership: Summary of Evidence Gathered from the Population of a Mutual Resident-Controlled Housing Association and Compared at Various Levels*. Submission of evidence to DCLG to support the Right to Transfer.

Rosenberg, Jonathan. 2013. *Widening the Door to Community Ownership – Right to Transfer: S34A Housing Act 1985 – Challenges and Opportunities*. Self-published report.

Sagoe, Cecil. 2016. 'One Tool Amongst Many: Considering the Political Potential of Neighbourhood Planning for the Greater Carpenters Neighbourhood, London', *Architecture, Media, Politics and Society* 9(3): 1–20.

Satsangi, Madhu and Murray, Susan. 2011. *Community Empowerment. Final Report to Walterton and Elgin Community Homes*. Stirling: University of Stirling.

Save Carpenters. https://savecarpenters.wordpress.com/about/. Accessed 28 February 2017.

Sendra, Pablo. 2018. 'Assemblages for Community-Led Social Housing Regeneration: Activism, Big Society and Localism', *City*, 22(5–6): 738–62.

Sendra, Pablo and Fitzpatrick, Daniel. 2018. 'Response to the Consultation Paper: Proposed New Funding Condition to Require Resident Ballots in Estate Regeneration'. Community-Led Social Housing Regeneration (9 April 2018). http://communityled.london/wp-content/uploads/2018/04/Response-to-ballot-consultation-PS-and-DF-UCL.pdf. Accessed 31 July 2019.

Sendra, Pablo and Fitzpatrick, Daniel. 2020. 'Time to Be an Activist: Recent Successes in London Housing Activism', in Susannah Bunce, Nicola Livingstone, Susan Moore and Alan Walks, eds., *Critical Dialogues of Urban Governance, Development and Activism: London & Toronto*. London: UCL Press.

Senior Court Act 1981, Section 31: Application for Judicial Review. http://www.legislation.gov.uk/ukpga/1981/54/section/31. Accessed 16 October 2019.

Skeffington, Arthur. 1969. *People and Planning. Report of the Committee on Public Participation in Planning*. HMSO: London.

Southwark Notes. 2019. 'Heygate Estate'. https://southwarknotes.wordpress.com/heygate-estate/. Accessed 19 July 2019.

Stavrides, Stavros. 2018. *Towards the City of Thresholds*. New York: Common Notions.

The Assets of Community Value (England) Regulations 2012. http://www.legislation.gov.uk/uksi/2012/2421/contents/made. Accessed 1 August 2019.

The Bartlett School of Planning, UCL. 2019. 'CPD Civic Design'. https://www.ucl.ac.uk/bartlett/planning/programmes/cpd-civic-design. Accessed 31 July 2019.

TheHousingForAll. 2013. *Housing 4 The Counihan's Housing 4 All!* (Documentary film, 2013). https://www.youtube.com/watch?time_continue=6&v=JgsGaCI1t-o. Accessed 30 July 2019.

The Housing (Right to Manage) Regulations 1994. http://www.legislation.gov.uk/uksi/1994/627/contents/made. Accessed 28 July 2019.

The Housing (Right to Manage) (England) Regulations 2008. http://www.legislation.gov.uk/uksi/2008/2361/contents/made. Accessed 28 July 2019.

The Housing (Right to Manage) (England) Regulations 2012. http://www.legislation.gov.uk/uksi/2012/1821/contents/made. Accessed 28 July 2019.

The National Lottery Community Fund. n.d. 'Parks for People'. https://www.tnlcommunityfund.org.uk/funding/programmes/parks-for-people#section-2. Accessed 27 July 2019.

The Neighbourhood Planning (General) Regulations 2012. http://www.legislation.gov.uk/uksi/2012/637/contents/made. Accessed 1 August 2019.

The Planning Inspectorate. 2019. 'Guide to Taking Part in Planning and Listed Building Consent Appeals Proceeding by an Inquiry – England' (September 2019). https://assets.publishing.service.gov.uk/government/uploads/system/uploads/attachment_data/file/832054/taking-part_planning-inquiry_September_2019.pdf. Accessed 16 October 2019.

Topal, Aylin, Yalman, Galip L. and Çelik, Özlem. 2019. 'Changing Modalities of Urban Redevelopment and Housing Finance in Turkey: Three Mass Housing Projects in Ankara', *Journal of Urban Affairs* 41(5): 630–53.

Town and Country Planning (Local Planning) Regulations 2012. http://www.legislation.gov.uk/uksi/2012/767/contents/made. Accessed 26 October 2019.

Transparency International UK. 2017. 'Faulty Towers: Understanding the Impact of Overseas Corruption on the London Property Market'. https://www.transparency.org.uk/publications/faulty-towers-understanding-the-impact-of-overseas-corruption-on-the-london-property-market. Accessed 10 May 2019.

Tuckett, Iain. 1988. 'Coin Street: There Is Another Way ...', *Community Development Journal* 23(4): 249–57.

UCL Engineering Exchange. 2017. 'Demolition or Refurbishment of Social Housing?' https://www.ucl.ac.uk/engineering-exchange/research-projects/2019/apr/demolition-or-refurbishment-social-housing. Accessed 1 August 2019.

UNECE Convention on Access to Information, Public Participation in Decision-Making and Access to Justice in Environmental Matters (Aarhus Convention, 1998). https://www.unece.org/fileadmin/DAM/env/pp/documents/cep43e.pdf. Accessed 16 October 2019.

Wainwright, Oliver. 2015. 'Revealed: How Developers Exploit Flawed Planning System to Minimise Affordable Housing', *The Guardian* (25 June 2015). https://www.theguardian.com/cities/2015/jun/25/london-developers-viability-planning-affordable-social-housing-regeneration-oliver-wainwright. Accessed 10 May 2019.

Wales, Robin. 2014. 'I Apologise to the Focus E15 Families, but This is a London Housing Crisis', *The Guardian* (6 October 2014). https://www.theguardian.com/commentisfree/2014/oct/06/apologise-focus-e15-london-housing-crisis-newham. Accessed 6 June 2017.

WECH (Walterton and Elgin Community Homes). 1999. *Against the Odds: Walterton and Elgin from Campaign to Control*. London: WECH.

WECH (Walterton and Elgin Community Homes). 2016. *Walterton & Elgin Community Homes Annual Report 2015/16*.

WECH (Walterton and Elgin Community Homes). n.d. 'How We Started'. http://wech.co.uk/company-who-we-are/about-us-who-we-are-what-we-do-etc/how-we-started.html. Accessed 18 November 2019.

Wates, Nick. 1976 [2013]. *The Battle for Tolmers Square*. London: Routledge Revivals.

Watt, Paul. 2016. 'A Nomadic War Machine in the Metropolis: En/countering London's 21st-Century Housing Crisis with Focus E15', *City* 20 (2): 297–320.

Index

Lightning Source UK Ltd.
Milton Keynes UK
UKHW020130091020
371248UK00002B/18